THE
BLASKET ISLANDS

'This beautifully produced book is a magnificent
monument to what was lost.'

BRENDAN KENNELLY, THE SUNDAY TRIBUNE

'... an enormous amount of material
has been gathered together within these covers relating
to such matters as the origins of the islanders, the families
who settled there, the trauma of the Famine days ... very
detailed descriptions of the Great Blasket village and the
intricate field system, descriptions of lesser islands, with a
whole range of pictures – including aerial shots – and
drawings covering almost every aspect of island life
... the authors have managed, through sheer study,
effort and dedication, to produce something of a
monumental work in its own field.'

THE EXAMINER

ALSO AVAILABLE

The Skellig Story
Des Lavelle

THE
BLASKET ISLANDS

NEXT PARISH AMERICA

Joan & Ray Stagles

THE O'BRIEN PRESS
DUBLIN

This revised edition first published 2006 by The O'Brien Press Ltd.,
20 Victoria Road, Dublin 6, Ireland.
Tel: +353 1 4923333; Fax: +353 1 4922777
E-mail: books@obrien.ie
Website: www.obrien.ie

First published in hardback 1980.
First paperback edition 1984.
Reprinted 1986, 1988. Revised 1998, 2006.

ISBN-10: 0-86278-973-7
ISBN-13: 978-0-86278-973-2

British Library Cataloguing-in-Publication Data
Stagles, Joan, d. 1978
The Blasket Islands: next parish America. - Rev. ed.
1.Blasket Islands (Ireland) - History 2. Blasket Islands
(Ireland) - Social life and customs
I.Title II.Stagles, Ray
941.9'6

7 8 9 10 11 12
06 07 08 09 10

Front cover photograph courtesy of Thomas Mason; back cover photograph George
Gmelch.

Cover design: Graham Thew
Printing: MPG Books Ltd

Contents

Illustrations

MAPS

Acknowledgements

(a note found in the papers of Joan Stagles)

For access to records and manuscripts, and for generous help and advice I am indebted to: Father Micheal Ó Ciosán of Ballyferriter for access to the parish registers; Mrs. Bridget Dolan, Librarian of the Royal Irish Academy, for access to manuscripts and for unstinted help and advice; Mrs. Peig Uí Dubhain, Librarian of Dingle Public Library; W. O'Sullivan, Keeper of Manuscripts, Trinity College Library, Dublin; the secretary and staff of the Department of Records of the Land Commission, Dublin; and the Director and the staff of the National Library, Dublin.

My grateful thanks are also due to all the island people for their hospitality, friendliness, and patience in supplying information and answering endless questions. It is to them that this book is dedicated.

The publishers wish to thank also Máire Ní Ghaoithín, Mícheál Ó Duláine, and Pádraig Ua Maoileoin for their help with Irish spellings. We are grateful to Mr. Harry MacMonagle, Donal O'Cahill, George Gmelch, Thomas Biuso, Kevin Danaher and all those who supplied illustrations. These are acknowledged below.

ILLUSTRATION SOURCES

We are grateful to the following who have supplied photographs and other illustrations for this book: Thomas N. Biuso (and Eibhlis Brett) page 42, (and Michael Camey) 102; Bord Fáilte 12; Clódhanna Teoranta (from *An Muircheartach*) 83; Commissioners of Public Works 24, 101, 119, 124; Dept. of Irish Folklore, UCD 37, 38, 41, 47, 49, 60, 77, 106, 111; *The Examiner*; 134; The Geological Survey 29, 62, 116, 117; George Gmelch 6, 16, 19, 20, 65, 69, 78, 93, 105, 114, 127; Dermot Mason and Thomas N. Biuso 93, 108; Thomas Mason 39, 51; Donal O'Cahill 32 (from Irish News Agency material) 10, 45, 55, 75 (by D. Mac Monagle); Daphne Pochin Mould 56, 73, 120; Syndics of Cambridge University Library 29; TCD (Synge collection) 35, 112; Michael Viney 123, 128; The Blasket Centre / Ionad an Bhlascaoid Mhóir 132. The maps and drawings are by Adrian Slattery based on material supplied by the authors and publisher.

Foreword to the fourth edition

It is now over a quarter of a century since my late wife Joan conducted the original research on which the bulk of this book is based. Since then more than 14,000 copies of the book have been sold.

The distinctive value of her work and the importance of her discoveries are demonstrated by the fact that they have been drawn on time and again in other books and television programmes that have appeared since. Only last summer a writer in the *Sunday Independent* said *The Blasket Islands – Next Parish America* is 'regarded as a definitive history of the islands'. This is claiming too much, but it is a gratifying acknowledgement of the quality and originality of Joan's research.

The final chapter in this edition is entirely new. In it I have attempted to bring the island's troubled story right up to date. It is my fervent hope that the major decisions made in 2005 will indeed usher in a glorious future for this extraordinarily beautiful and historic Irish island.

Ray Stagles
January 2006

Preface to the first edition

My wife Joan and I first visited the Great Blasket Island in July 1966, and then returned year after year to camp there each summer until her failing health made that impossible. The island, its people and its history quickly became her dominant interest. It led her to seek out ex-islanders in Dunquin and further afield, to learn Irish, and to spend many happy days in research at the British Museum, in Dublin, and on the Dingle Peninsula, making very many good friends in the process. The heart of this book – chapters 2 to 8 – is the fruit of her labours over a period of twelve years, until her sudden death in July 1978. She was always revising what she had written, as she came across some fresh detail, either in books or in old newspapers, or through correspondence and conversation with Blasket Island people and their friends. These seven she had completed more or less to her satisfaction, and I have edited them hardly at all.

What sort of book is this? Perhaps it is easier to start by saying what it is not. It is emphatically not a digest of all the other Blasket Island books that have already appeared in print. The original island autobiographies and letters are so fine and vivid and personal that there can be no substitute for reading them if you wish to learn anything about the nature of the Blasket Island community. What this book essentially attempts to do is to fill out the historical background to that community in areas that have hitherto been little explored. It is, in fact, like Robin Flower's book, *The Western Island*, a collection of essays; but, again, it deliberately avoids repeating what he said, and instead highlights matters that he did not touch on. This book, then, is another addition to what George Thomson, the translator of *Twenty Years A-Growing*, called "the Blasket Library"; it includes much original material. However, there are further rich seams yet to be mined (e.g. through careful archaeological study) and we can all look forward, I am sure, to further Blasket Island books.

Ray Stagles

Editor's Note on Irish spellings: There is considerable variation in the spellings of the Blasket Islands, with as many as six different spellings for Inishvickillaune alone. The spellings of Inis Tuaisceart, Inis na Bró, Beiginis, and Tearacht used here are given in Irish. The recognised Irish spelling of Inishvickillaune is Inis Mhic Fhaoláin, but we chose to use the former, equally accepted spelling, since it will be more familiar to most readers. An Blascaod Mór is given in English since it is so widely known as the Great Blasket.

Dunmore Head with Great Blasket in the distance.

1
Next Parish America

The mountain and coastal scenery of the Dingle Peninsula is bold and grand throughout. As soon as you pass through Blennerville on the outskirts of Tralee and strike straight to the west, you find yourself in a magnificent region of bare mountain and sweeping coastline that cries out to you that it is leading you to the uttermost edges of Europe. And when, over forty miles further on, having crossed the mountain ridge that is the backbone of the peninsula, you come to that final stretch of coast from Slea Head to Ballydavid Head — "next parish America" — the grandeur of that final scatter of islands at the opening to 3,000 miles of Atlantic Ocean is overwhelming. There, at the centre of the group, is the Great Blasket Island, worthy of its name in every way.

The geological formations that underlie this peninsula are as bold and straightforward as the landscape itself. Folds of Old Red Sandstone and allied rocks extend in a direct east-west line, limited to the south in the Slieve Mish Mountains only by even older pre-Devonian rocks. As for the Blasket Group itself, "high ridges of purple sandstone, similar to those of the mainland, have been isolated from the rest of the Dingle Peninsula by marine encroachment".[1] In the nearly 1,000 foot northern cliff of the Great Blasket Island, aptly named "Fatal Cliff", one sees a continuation of the even higher cliffs of Sauce Creek on the mainland, and in the gentler grassy slopes of *an Pháirc* on the south side of the island, one is reminded of the gentle decline down the southern Saints Road from the heights of Mount Brandon. At this far western end of Europe there is not a copse of trees anywhere on island or mainland to break the pure line of mountain and hill, silhouetted against sky and sea on every side.

From whatever direction you approach this most westerly point of the Dingle Peninsula and County Kerry, whether you come along the southern coastal road round Slea Head, or from the north by Clogher, or over the mountain road from Ventry to Dunquin which cuts between Mount Eagle and Croagh Martin, your first sight of the Blasket Islands is likely to give your heart a sudden jerk which is both painful and ecstatic. On the coast road from Dingle to Dunquin, the route most visitors take, you can catch glimpses of Inishvickillaune

(Inisvickilaun), but the shoulder of Mount Eagle conceals the rest of the Blasket group until, as you swing round Slea Head, the whole cluster of islands is dramatically revealed, floating in the Atlantic like a school of basking whales, hump-backed all of them, except for little Beiginis which lies nearest inshore as flat as a jelly-fish.

There are days, when, from the coast road, the Great Blasket looks so close you could reach out and touch its field walls and broken houses and stroke the grass on its muscular mountain slopes. There are other days when the great island shrinks to half the size and withdraws itself far out into the Atlantic, aloof, and infinitely untouchable. At all times this island has an appearance of mysterious self-containment and otherness, totally at odds with the visible relics of human occupation and cultivation.

For some people an island exerts an irresistible attraction. Many have felt the pull of the Great Blasket long before they actually saw it, for the Blasket — out of all the Irish islands, and there are said to be over 300 of them — has been specially blessed with a small but vigorous population of distinctive character and intelligence with outstanding literary gifts. Not one but three autobiographies, as well as other books, each one highly individual in flavour, came out of this island within the space of seven years (between 1929 and 1936). They are acknowledged classics of the Irish language, and widely read in translation too. This is a remarkable achievement for such a tiny and isolated peasant community. The Aran Islands, their people, their stony fields, their legends and antiquities have been rightly celebrated by Synge and by scholars from all over Europe. But what island has been so vibrantly portrayed, from the inside, by its own people as the Blasket? Some of the Scottish islands, the Orkneys in particular, have produced distinguished poets and writers, but most of these have been mainland educated, comparatively sophisticated and open to wide cultural influences. Nowhere else in Britain or Ireland has a small island produced a literary flowering to compare with that of the Blasket, rooted so deeply in its indigenous peasant culture and thrusting up so vigorous and sinewy. What makes the Blasket literature even more remarkable is the fact that it arose from an isolated community which at its peak, during the First World War, numbered little more than 160 men, women and children.

Many people have come to know and relish the peculiarly salty, violent, gentle, philosophical, lyrical, sardonic, devout, blasphemous, comic, tragic flavour of the Blasket community from the writings of Tomás Ó Criomhthain, Maurice Ó Sullivan, and Peig Sayers, as well as from a number of later island writers. The island's place names, the style of its houses and its boats, the names and character of some of its people, with their great talk, tales and music, are thus familiar, while

Map 1
Blasket Islands
Location Map

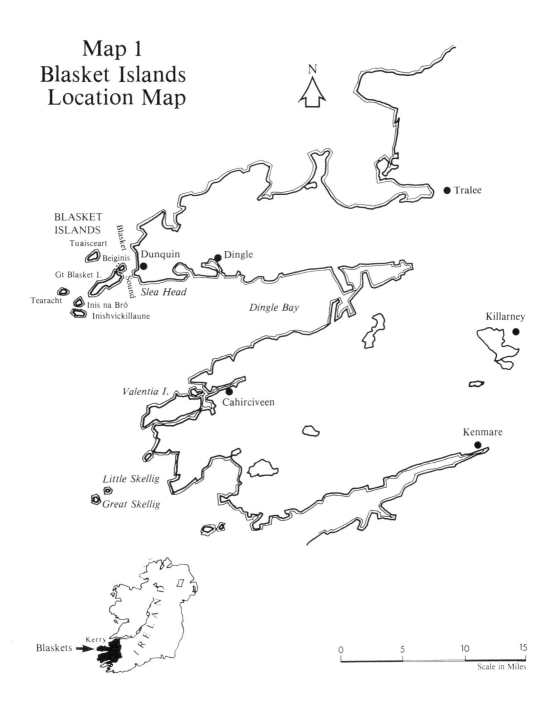

N

Tralee

BLASKET
ISLANDS

Tuaisceart

Beiginis   Dunquin   Dingle

Gt Blasket I.

Blasket Sound

Tearacht

Inis na Bró   Slea Head
Inishvickillaune

Dingle Bay

Killarney

Valentia I.

Cahirciveen

Kenmare

Little Skellig

Great Skellig

IRELAND

Blaskets ➤ Kerry

0   5   10   15

Scale in Miles

Naomhógs at Dunquin Harbour.

at the same time strange, to the visitors who come from all over the world to gaze at the Blasket from the mainland, or to embark on a day trip to the island from the tiny harbour at Dunquin.

When we first came to the island in 1966 it had been abandoned for thirteen years, and most of the village houses were roofless shells; but a few were still maintained by the last half-dozen island families, now re-housed on the nearby mainland. The condition of the village then would have broken the heart of anyone who had known it in earlier days. We have seen the bewilderment and shock of island people who have returned after thirty or forty years in America, when confronted with the wreckage of their old home.

Yet the island had not been totally deserted. A subdued, crepuscular life continued intermittently. During the spring and summer, and in quiet spells during the winter, most of the islandmen made occasional trips across the sound to fish, carry day-trippers, or tend the sheep which they continued to graze on the island throughout the year. Several, whose roots went particularly deep, regularly spent a considerable part of each summer in residence in their old homes, on a sort of working holiday not unlike the old Irish tradition of the *buaile,* the "booley" or summer farm, when the young people would take the cattle and sheep up to hill pastures as soon as spring came out and stay with them in lightly-built temporary dwellings throughout the summer months. During the day they clipped and doctored their sheep, fished, went rabbiting, painted and repaired their houses, tarred roofs, cut and stacked turf, gathered driftwood, and, in the evening, gossiped at the well, brewed strong tea, talked and smoked tobacco round one fire or another. Sometimes the background was filled with traditional music from a transistor radio towards which loyal and critical ears would be bent in intense concentration whenever the island poet, Mike Peig Sayers, or some other local personality was being broadcast on Radio na Gaeltachta. If this was only a grey shadow of the old social life of the island — the *cuideachtan* and *céilidhe* of younger days when people gathered for story, song and dance — it still had the living voice and idiosyncratic character of the true Blasket community.

It was our good fortune to reach the island while a handful of the last island-born people remained in the area, including one or two outstanding personalities born in the eighties of the last century. And it was still possible to locate the setting of events and conversations recorded in the Blasket memoirs. To many literary pilgrims, ourselves included, the Blasket Island is hallowed ground. It was a significant experience to cross Tomás Ó Criomhthain's threshold; to stand by the hearth of Seán Lís Ó Sullivan where young Maurice noted, on his first day home, the glowing fire, the four *sugán* chairs with seats of straw rope, and the dog lying among the ashes; or to retrace the path by which Peig Sayers walked from her father-in-law's house to visit Cait Ní Bhriain, the weaver's wife, by way of the little stone-pit where Micí Diarmada saw the ghost, down the "Little Road of the Dead" and up by the corner of the "White Field" (discovering, as one does not from the book, that this is a curiously roundabout route which raises interesting questions not only about Micí Diarmada, but about the reason for not taking the direct path to the weaver's door).

"I would love it if you had come to the island when we were living there," said an island friend. "It was a little small house I was born in and reared on the island. I wish we were young there again ..." The tides rise and fall regularly according to their pattern, but each tide is a new one, washing up new debris, washing away old footprints. Old walls fall in, old paths are overgrown. The details which were once distinct become obscured and then forgotten.

The physical geography of the Great Blasket permitted a permanent community of less than 200, and yet even so there was an acute shortage of arable land. No family held more than three or four acres capable of cultivation; most had much less. All were forced to eke out a living from a variety of sources – fishing, fowling, salvage from the sea and contributions from exiled relatives in America. The poverty, isolation and perpetual hazards of sea and weather imposed a high degree of mutual dependence and a strong sense of communal identity as the *lucht an Oileáin* ("island people") – a people distinct from those on the mainland, though closely allied to them by blood and marriage.

A nice balance between private and communal life existed in the island of which the system of sheep-farming is an example. Most of the island consists of rough unfenced mountain land which was used as common grazing. The task of rounding up and separating one's own sheep from those of others would have been almost impossible on one's own. The backbone ridge of the island tips steeply down to the sea on both edges – like a church roof as botanist R. L. Praeger once aptly described it. Thus, over the years, the island men evolved a system of co-operative lambing, shearing, tallying, and marking. Enough of this system survived twenty years after the evacuation of the island, which took place in 1953, to show that it must originally have been fairly complex. In the early 1960s a party of six or more would go over to the island in the spring, and together round up all the sheep over the whole island, clip each lamb's ears in the same pattern as its ewe's, shear and dip the sheep together, and take the wool back to the mainland for sale.

After more than twenty years on the mainland some of the former islanders' traditional ties with the island are loosening, partly because they are less relevant to present circumstances, partly because age and death have broken important links in the human chain. Nevertheless,

The Great Blasket, left, and Tuaisceart, right, from Slea Head.

An over-grown roadway leads to the village.

the sense of identity, the consciousness of belonging to the island and of being bound by particular loyalties is still very strong. So, too, is a pride, unassuming and unpretentious though it is, in the island and the achievements of its writers (often coupled, as within a family, with sardonic allusions to their personal inadequacies). There is, too, a deep regret for the passing of the island-born community. This is not just nostalgia and regret for lost youth, though this is part of it; it is more a recognition that the dying of this intensely Gaelic community signifies the loss of something which was once, but is no longer, vital to Ireland's national identity. Tomás Ó Criomhthain's prophetic words haunt the mind: "The like of us will not be seen again."

(*Note to the third edition, 1998:* This final paragraph refers specifically to the position in 1980. Most of the former islanders whose views and feelings it refers to are, sadly, now dead; and those who remain rarely, if ever, make the journey across the Blasket Sound to their old island home. But they are always delighted to hear reports of "how things are there" nowadays.)

Map 2
Blasket Island Group

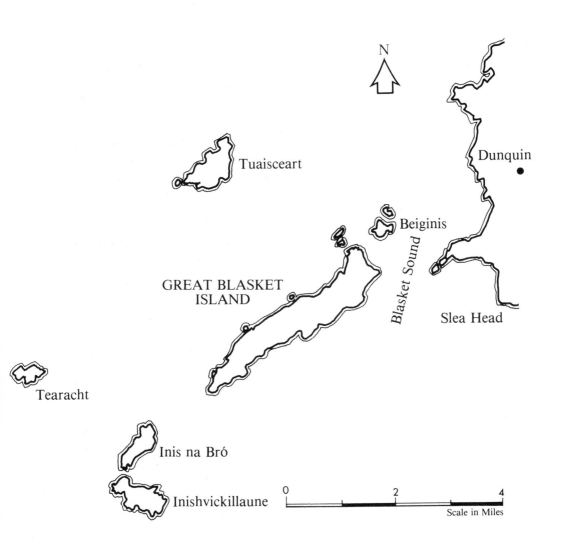

N

Tuaisceart

Dunquin

Beiginis

GREAT BLASKET
ISLAND

Blasket Sound

Slea Head

Tearacht

Inis na Bró

Inishvickillaune

0   2   4
Scale in Miles

2
Origins
of the
Island
Community

The village which lies above the landing place is a straggling affair scattered over a steep and lumpy hillside. There is hardly a square yard of level ground here except on the narrow cliff top and on one or two small headlands. There is little evidence to tell how long this village site was inhabited. The "ruins of a very ancient church" mentioned by Charles Smith in 1756 have long since vanished, although ironically, this church is still listed as an Ancient Monument.[2] The old stone cross which once stood near the well on the south side of the village had disappeared by the middle of the last century; the only remaining trace of it is in the name it gave to the well, *Tobar na Croise* ("Well of the Cross"). The island-born chronicler, Tomás Ó Criomhthain, wrote in 1933: "There was a stone cross to be seen standing above this well in the old days, but I don't remember ever seeing the cross myself. It fell down, like many another of its kind."[3] Possibly it found its way into the masonry of one of the island houses or field walls. The cross and ancient church suggest the possibility that the village site may have held some medieval settlement, either religious or secular, but there are no buildings left at the village site today which can be identified with certainty as more than two centuries old.

There are, however, relics of unmistakably ancient buildings further west: a small ring fort, probably from the Iron Age, and a number of clocháns (stone beehive huts). A dún, or fort, stands at the very edge of the 900 foot northern escarpment which rears above the formidable Lochar rocks. The first edition of the six-inch Ordnance Survey map, published in 1841, shows two complete rings side by side. But what appears today are two semi-circular areas, enclosed by rubble and earth walls. Possibly parts of the mounds have been lost in cliff falls. One tradition in the island associates the Dún with the Danes, and in view of the fact that this coast, including the monastery on Sceilig Mhichil, was raided by the Vikings, it is possible that the sea raiders may have taken over and used this eyrie as a camp and lookout over the northern approaches. But they did not build the fort, which must have been centuries old when they arrived.

About a mile and a half still further west are traces of several

Stone remains on Inis Tuaisceart.

clochan clusters on a gently rolling slope known as the Red Ridge *(an Drom Rua)*. This is the first of the three great steps by which the island drops from the peak of the Cro at 961 feet to the remote western point called the Black Head *(Ceann Dubh)*. The remains of most of the clocháns are so fragmentary that it is difficult to say precisely how many there were originally. In certain lights over a dozen circles can be counted in the grass, but only two have any amount of wall left standing. The clocháns are grouped in two clusters, one on the north and one on the south of the ridge. These remote stone huts are called by the island people *na Clocháin Gheala* ("the Bright Dwellings"). They may have been associated with an early Christian monastic settlement, like the similar but better preserved structures on the nearby islands of Inishvickillaune and Inis Tuaisceart, and, a little further away, Sceilig Mhichil. There are no identifiably religious remains to be seen here, however, no graves, crosses or traditions of religious relics, apart from the vanished church and cross near the village already mentioned. Although the actual distance between the clocháns and the village is less than three miles, the mountainous terrain makes this a considerable and troublesome distance. The islanders have no traditions relating to the builders or inhabitants of the *Clocháin Gheala,* except of a very general kind, that "they belonged to the people long ago".

From various legal documents we know that by the thirteenth century the Great Blasket was leased to the Ferriter family by the Earl of Desmond, to whom they paid an annual rent of two hawks. The island remained in the possession of the Ferriters until the end of the Desmond rebellion in 1583. The forfeited lands of the rebel were then allotted in 1586 to supporters of the Crown or to English Protestant planters. According to Charles Smith, the Blaskets were granted to two English adventurers named Stone and Champion, and eventually, by various sales, came into the possession of Sir Richard Boyle, later the Earl of Cork. They remained part of the extensive Cork and Orrery estate until November 1907 when the Great Blasket was bought by the Congested Districts Board and freeholds were sold to the tenant-occupiers.

Maps and documents from the sixteenth and seventeenth centuries often refer to the Blaskets as "Ferriter's Islands". The only member of the family who is remembered in the Blasket folk tradition, however, is Pierce *(Pieras)* Ferriter, the poet-rebel who was executed in Killarney in 1641. He is credited with possessing both a castle and a cave on the island. Both places are associated with feats of daring and endurance. *Scairt Phiarais* ("Pierce's Cave") is near the bottom of the steep and dangerous 900 foot scarp known as "Fatal Cliff" which hangs between the two peaks of the island, *an Cró Mór* and *Sliabh an Dúna*. It is almost impossible to locate this cave without a guide. The descent is so long and steep that even the sure-footed islandmen would not attempt it now, though they knew it well as boys. The story of Pierce's hardships and the verse he is said to have composed in this cave are well known to readers of the island books, particularly *Twenty Years A-Growing* and *The Western Island*.

According to tradition, Ferriter's Castle — neither built nor owned by Ferriter himself — was sited a little to the north of the island's landing place, on a small headland known as *Rinn a' Chaisleáin* ("Castle Point") part of which was used by islanders as an unconsecrated graveyard where unbaptised infants, shipwrecked sailors and one sad suicide are buried. Tomás Ó Criomhthain records that tooled masonry, which is not normally found in Blasket houses, was once uncovered when a grave was being dug there. There seems to be enough supporting evidence to indicate that there once was some type of defensive structure here, whether from the Ferriter period or earlier. Systematic archaeological investigation, however, is needed to establish the facts. It is unlikely that the Ferriters were ever in regular residence on the island, but they may have used the castle as a hunting lodge, and perhaps kept a small garrison here in times of trouble. Any kind of tower or fortification on this headland must have been conspicuous from the seaward side. The fact that there is no mention of the castle in the journal kept by the captain of one of the Armada ships that anchored just off the island for nearly a week in 1588 suggests that it was already in ruins, perhaps destroyed, by government troops after the Desmond rebellion.

The Blaskets, being so inaccessible, small and economically and strategically unimportant, attracted little attention from official recorders or historians until the present century. Even the local newspapers published in Tralee throughout the nineteenth century informed their readers more about events in Dublin, Westminster, Europe, and the Far East than they did about anything happening west of Dingle. News of the Queen and the British Royal Family was a regular weekly feature, but you can search through several years' small print without finding a single reference to the Blaskets. If Dingle itself was remote and foreign to the civilised people of Tralee, then the Blaskets lay on the very edge of the known world. Only when by some rare combination of fortuitous circumstances the circles of local affairs intersected those of national or international interest did the islands receive much documentation, as in 1588 — the year of the Armada wrecks.

Aramburo's journal and the eyewitness accounts of those aboard the Armada ships are disappointingly uninformative about the Blasket Islands. The Spanish Admiral, Recalde, sent a boat to the Great Blasket each day "to refresh themselves and to take water", but could do so, as Aramburo reports, "but little and that with much labour".[4] Why?

Inishvickillaune, Inis na Bró and the Great Blasket Island – from left to right.

Was their difficulty due to bad weather or the problems of landing? There are several small wells along the eastern coastline of the island; there could have been no shortage of water at that season. Could the Spanish have encountered hostility from the islanders? The native Irish were generally sympathetic towards the Spaniards. Moreover, the Spanish were fighting men, however weakened by sickness and privation. Was the Blasket even inhabited at the time?

The fact that Aramburo does not mention inhabitants does not necessarily mean that there were none. More decisive, perhaps, is a reference contained in a letter from the Venetian ambassador in Madrid to the wrecking of one of the Armada ships in "an uninhabited Irish port".[5] The ship concerned sank in the Blasket Sound. The uninhabited port may or may not refer to the "haven of Vicey" (the name Aramburo gives to Recalde's anchorage – presumed to lie off the White Strand), and therefore to the Blasket Island itself. The phrase, based on second or third-hand information, must be treated with caution.

The earliest direct reference to island inhabitants does not come until 1736 when the sixth Earl of Cork, an absentee landowner, visited his extensive estates in Ireland, of which the Blaskets and other parts of *Corca Dhuibhne* were the remotest parts, for the first time. Standing on the mainland he reported seeing:

some tillage and a few cabins, from whence, during the Time I was looking at the Island, some poor Wretches entered into a Boat with Rabbits for Sale. Nothing, sure, but Necessity could

Map 3
Great Blasket Island

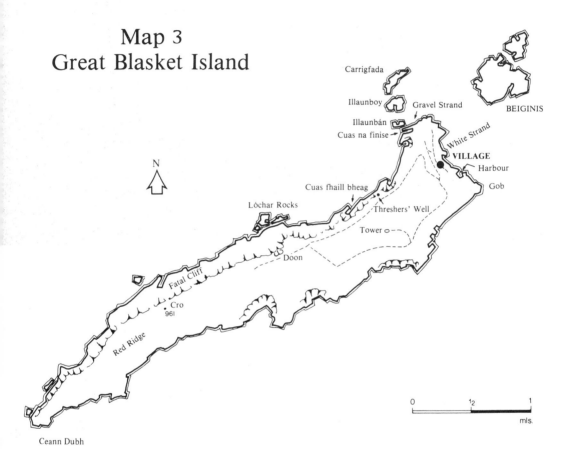

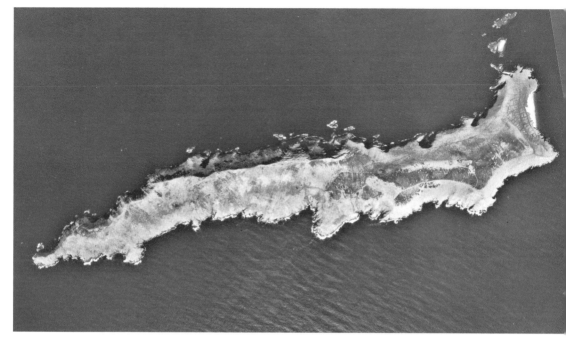

The Great Blasket from 15,000 feet.

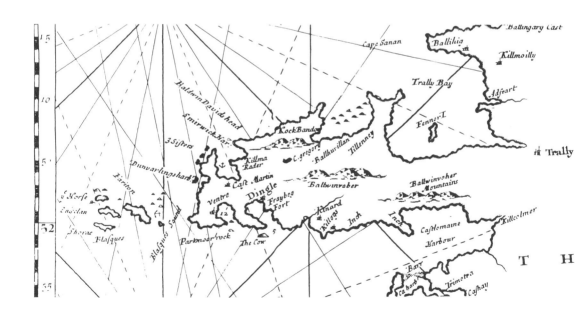

A sixteenth century map of the Dingle Peninsula.

force 'em to trust to so tempestuous a sea, the sight of which shock'd me so much that I hastened to Ballyferriter, but not without leaving my hearty Prayers for the Rabbit Merchants.[6]

Nearly twenty years later Charles Smith travelled to Dingle, and perhaps also to Dunquin and other villages to the west, collecting material for his monumental work *Ancient and Present State of the County of Kerry,* published in 1756. Although he compiled a substantial amount of information about the Blaskets, it is clear that he received it at second hand from informants on the mainland.

The island called Innismore, i.e. the great island, is about three miles in length. It hath an high mountain, with some arable land towards the North East end; five or six families reside on it, who pay tithes to a very distant parish called Ballinvohir. The inhabitants are strong, lusty and healthy, and, what is very surprising, neither man, woman or child died on it for the space of forty-five years before I was there, although several persons who, during that period, came over to the main land, fell sick and died out of the island almost in sight of their usual abode. Somewhat like this salubrity of the air, is also mentioned on the western isles of Scotland.[7]

The details about the geography of the island and the number of families may be taken as fact, but remarks about the longevity of the islanders clearly have the flavour of after-dinner tattle among country gentlemen or lawyers, the sort of people to whom eighteenth century travellers would normally carry letters of introduction. The islanders had evidently acquired a legendary quality by this time. "Forty-five years before I was there" carries us back to some time between 1700 and 1710 but by inference it takes us back a good deal further, since the rest of the quotation implies that the Blasket had a settled community previous to that time during which people had died on the island. Certainly it suggests that the Blasket people had been there long enough to have become distinct and remarkable, and to have acquired a reputation for health and long life. Smith's remarks, taken with the negative evidence from the Armada period, suggest the establishment − possibly the re-establishment − of a small settlement on the Great Blasket some time during the seventeenth century.

The site of this small settlement, at the eastern end of the island, was clearly identical with that of the village we know today. It is, in fact, the only rational site for a permanent settlement for anyone other than ascetics or hermits. It has a number of basic assets: several springs of fresh water; shelter from the prevailing west winds; and the greater part of the island's small area of arable land close at hand. In addition, it is located at the point closest to the mainland, a factor important for both psychological and physical reasons. A small off-shore island such as the Blasket cannot easily be totally independent and self-sufficient, and there are few island dwellers who do not find some re-assurance in the lights of a mainland village across the dark strait. The main drawback of the village site is the steepness of the slope, which created problems for both builders and residents.

The "few cabins" noted by the Earl of Cork, and Smith's "five or six families" suggest that the Blasket community in the mid-eighteenth century was a small one. But exactly how small? We do not know whether Smith meant five or six married couples with their children (nuclear families), or five or six extended families, nor do we know how many generations may have been living together in each of the few cabins. The traditional "family" meaning an extended group of several generations with branches and off-shoots linked through the male line was the prevailing form in the Irish countryside at that time and much later. With this in mind, the Blasket settlement of 1736-56 may well have been considerably larger than one would expect using the elementary or nuclear family as a basis for calculations. The popula-tion of this period might well have been around fifty or sixty, rather than twenty or thirty.

The sudden rise in population which began in Ireland during the second half of the eighteenth century also occurred in *Corca Dhuibhne* and on the Great Blasket. It resulted in a movement of population out-ward from the mainland onto the Great Blasket, and from the Great Blasket itself to the remoter, smaller islands of the Blasket group, particularly Inishvickillaune and Inis Tuaisceart, and to a lesser degree, Beiginis and Inis na Bró. Both Smith and the Earl of Cork state categorically that the Great Blasket was the only island of the group which was inhabited at the time of their visits. "There have been none here for many years past," Smith wrote of Inishvickillaune.[8] However, by 1808 there was at least one family of Guiheens living on Inishvickillaune, and by 1817 there was a family on Inis Tuaisceart. These dates come from the baptismal registers of the parish of Ferriter, a large parish which included Dunquin, the Blaskets and most of the villages at the western end of the Dingle peninsula north and west of Ventry. The register was not begun until 1808 so it does not tell us how long the Guiheens have been on Inishvickillaune, but it is clear from the number of entries between 1808 and 1895 relating to the smaller islands that there was a continual colonising movement of families from the Great Blasket to the outer islands. The population of the Great Blasket Island is given in the official census of 1821 as 128, living in eighteen houses; by 1841 the population had risen to 153. During and after the Great Famine (1846-50) the population fell again, though the drop was proportionately less severe than in many of main-land parishes.

The last Blasket child, Gearoid Ó Catháin, with his grandfather outside their new home.

3
The
Island
Families

During the first ten years (1808-17) covered by baptismal register relating to all the Blasket islands, only eight family names occur. Two names, Burke and Sheehy, occur only once and then disappear entirely from the Blasket entries. The remaining names, which include sixteen different family units (two of which may be remarriages), are in order of appearance: Kearney (Ó Cheárna) — one family; Geehan or Guiheen (Ó Guithín) — five families; Donlea or Dunlevy (Ó Dhuinnshléibhe) — two families; Shea (Ó Séaghdha, Ó Sé) — three families; Crohan or MacCrohan (Ó Criomhthain) — two families; Kean, Kane or Keane (Ó Catháin) — one family. These six names occur regularly in the Blasket entries throughout the nineteenth century and into the twentieth, heavily outnumbering all others. It does not seem unreasonable to conclude that these are the names of the "five or six families" mentioned by Smith in 1756.

Sixteen additional Blasket surnames occur in the baptismal registers at various times during the nineteenth century, most of them before 1840. Of these, only three became established island surnames — O'Connor (Ó Conchúbhair) and O'Sullivan (Ó Suilleabháin) which first appear in 1831 and 1838 respectively; and Daly (Ó Dála) which appears first in 1860. Like the Burke and the Sheehy families, already mentioned, most of the others appear to have been birds of passage who stayed only long enough to baptise one, sometimes two, children in the islands. They may have been mainlanders who joined island families as sons-in-law but eventually moved back to the mainland, or they may have been new couples from the mainland temporarily trying island life during periods of stress.

Baptismal registers alone give only a partial, and possibly misleading, impression of the state of the population. Other sources such as family traditions must also be taken into consideration. The O'Sullivan family provides an interesting example. The first O'Sullivan does not occur in the island's baptismal entries until 1838, but oral tradition suggests that the first member of the family actually moved onto the island some thirty years earlier, leaving Cnan in Ventry parish after a widespread eviction by the landlord.[9] The story as told by

Eoghan Mór, Maurice O'Sullivan's grandfather, describes how Eoghan's father, Michael, was in the island working on the road which later would lead to the Signal Tower. If Eoghan's story is correct, his father must have moved onto the island not later than 1808, despite the fact that his first recorded child was not baptised until 1838. His wife's name at this date (1838) is given as Maria Donlea (Máire Ní Duinnshléibhe). For some reason, at least two children of this marriage (Eoghan and Michil) do not appear in the register at all. The story is further complicated by Michael O'Sullivan's remarriage late in life. His second wife (or possibly his third) was Catherine Granfield (known as Cáit Bhilly). Five children of this marriage are recorded in the baptismal register. The last one was baptised in 1879, by which time Michael O'Sullivan must have reached a considerable age, as confirmed in Tomás Ó Criomhthain's story about island girls making fun of an elderly husband and father. (Tomás also records that Michael O'Sullivan was a poet, though less of his verse has survived than that of his younger contemporary, Sean Ó Dhuinnshléibhe.)

The first O'Connors recorded in the baptismal register, Timothy and his wife Margaret Dunleih (Dhuinnshléibhe), had five children baptised between 1831 and 1852. This, however, may not represent the full extent of their family, for there is a curious gap of eleven years between the last two recorded children. This time span (1841-52) covers a much longer period than the years of the Great Famine which so greatly reduced the birthrate in Ferriter parish. It may be significant that these eleven years fall roughly within the period of Protestant influence on the Blasket, from about 1839 to 1850. We know from various sources that Tim O'Connor and his family were, or became, Protestants, and that they remained so (unlike several other families who "jumped" for a brief period during the worst years of the famine). This could account for some of the omissions in the Ferriter register. Some children may have been baptised by the Protestant clergy of Ventry (or Dingle) during the ten years following the opening of the "Soupers" school on the Blasket in 1840.

For a year during 1834 and 1835, the O'Connors attempted to farm the thirty-acre island of Beiginis which lies between the Great Blasket and the mainland. Early in the nineteenth century a large house had been built there by the Earl of Cork's agent to serve as a "milk house" or dairy. Three other families attempted to settle on the island during the first half of the nineteenth century, but only for short periods. For although Beiginis is fertile, it has no springs. Water had to be fetched by boat from the main island, resulting on one occasion in a fatal accident. The fact that the O'Connors were living in Beiginis for a time is revealed in a census of the parish of Ferriter compiled, probably in January 1855, by Father John Casey. The baptismal register shows

*Blasket islanders as photographed by J. M. Synge in 1905. From left to right —
Michael Keane, Nellie Keane, Michael Guiheen, Thomas Dunleavy, James Dunleavy,
Maurice Keane, "King" Patrick Keane, Mary Keane and Kate Keane.*

that the O'Connors had a child (John) baptised on 29 June 1834, and another (Maurice) on 24 September 1835. In both cases the place of residence is given as "Blasket". It would seem, then, that the O'Connors must have moved into and out of Beiginis between those two dates. Indeed, they had probably moved out of Beiginis early in 1835, for Father Casey's original entry giving the O'Connor's townland as Beiginis is deleted and amended "Island", meaning the Great Blasket. The number of people in the O'Connor household is given as seven (three males, four females). Only two children, both boys, are recorded in the baptismal registers at this date. One child of this family, Eoghan Bhán, later became a weaver in the Blasket, setting up his loom in the abandoned schoolroom of the Soupers, described by J. M. Synge as "a sort of outhouse with a damp feeling in the air".[10] Synge visited the Blasket in 1904 and left a description of the weaver as "old" and "looking pale and sickly compared with the other islanders". Synge was struck by the fine, undyed colour and quality of the flannel woven from selected wools from the black and speckled sheep then common on the island. The cloth was sent to Dingle for finishing and making up. Eoghan Bhán (the only weaver the island ever had) is also remembered in the literature for his association with Maurice O'Sullivan's school friend, Tomás Eoghain Bháin ("grandson of Fair-haired Eugene"). O'Connor (Ó Conchúbhair) is a fairly common name throughout *Corca Dhuibhne,* and the epithet "bán" ("white") associated with O'Connor occurs in several localities on the mainland in the lists of householders given by the Irish writer An Seabhac in *Treocha-Céad Chorca Dhuibhne,* which is based on the Griffith Valuation of 1850. It is very probable that these were members of the same family; it can hardly be mere coincidence that the epithet "bán" occurs over a dozen times in association with this surname, but only once with any other name. Seven of these "bán" O'Connors lived in various townlands in Ventry parish, two each in the parishes of Dunurlin and Marhin, one in Dunquin and one in Cloghane. On this evidence it would appear that the family originated in the Ventry area.

The name Daly came comparatively late to the Blaskets, although several Daly women had earlier married island men. The first recorded marriage, of Mary Daly to Donal Crohan, took place as early as 1811. Around 1860, Maurice Daly of Baile an Ghleanna married Catherine Guithín, a daughter of the family that farmed Inishvickillaune. This couple settled first in the Great Blasket where they had five children, all baptised between 1860 and 1873.[11] In late 1873 or early 1874, they moved to lonely Inishvickillaune. Maurice Daly took over his brother-in-law's homestead. (Seán Mheraigh Guiheen had recently drowned and his wife and family were forced to leave the island.) Three more children were born to Maurice and Catherine Daly in 1876,

1880 and 1882. Despite their isolated situation, it is clear from Tomás Ó Criomhthain's stories of the island that the Dalys were a very sociable, hospitable family. They remained on the island until 1903 or 1904 when, with most of the children having emigrated, the old people and one son moved back to the Great Blasket where their son and grandsons remained until the final evacuation of that island in 1953. The deeply ingrained island character of this family is illustrated in Synge's story about the original Maurice Daly, who, as an old man, could not bear to leave the Inis even for the Great Blasket.

> Then they told me about an old man of eighty years, who is going to spend the winter alone on Inishvickillaune, an island six miles from this village. His son is making canoes and doing other carpenter's jobs on this island, and the other children have scattered also; but the old man refuses to leave the island he has spent his life on, so they have left him with a goat, and a bag of flour and stack of turf.[12]

Synge clearly supposed the old man to have been born and bred on the inish, and it is interesting to see how little consciousness is shown, even by native Blasket writers, of Big Maurice Daly's mainland origin.

How many of the "strangers" (non-islanders) shared houses with relatives or lodged with island families, and how many became householders in their own right we do not know, but it is interesting to note

Two Blasket islanders, photographed in 1924 by Prof. von Sydow.

37

Islanders persuade a cow into a naomhóg for transport to the mainland, circa 1930.

Tomás Ó Criomhthain in 1929 holding a copy of his book
'An tOileánach' (The Islandman).

that at the time of the Griffith Valuation Survey in 1850 all seventeen householders on the Great Blasket and one on Inishvickillaune — the other islands were unoccupied at this time — carried regular island names. (The situation might have been different if the survey had been carried out nine years earlier. Then the main island had ten additional occupied houses, and a population of 153, compared with only 97 in 1851.) Similarly, in the Earl of Cork's last rental list in 1893-1894 all twenty tenants had regular island surnames. The Congested Districts Board's list of the twenty-nine householders compiled in 1917 shows only two additional names on the Blasket; one was that of the Daly family who had moved in from Inishvickillaune and the other was Thomas Savage, the National School master.

Sullivans, O'Connors and Dalys thus formed the core of the island community together with the six older families: Kearneys, Keanes, Guiheens, Dunleavys, Crithins and O'Sheas. Other surnames found among the Blasket baptismal entries include Burke, Moriarty, Fitzgerald, Manning, Moran, Landers, Grandfield, Sheehy, Kavan (or Kavanagh), Moore, Murphy, O'Brien and Hannafin. Most of these occur before the Great Famine. Of these families, only four had more than two children on the islands, which may indicate the length of time spent there.

Apart from the Dalys discussed above, only three new surnames occur in the baptismal registers after 1850. They are: Landers, Grandfield and Hannafin. Maurice Landers and Catherine Guiheen had one child, baptised in 1859. William Grandfield and Mary Keane had four children between 1860 and 1867. In both these families the wife was an island girl. In the following decade, however, we find an interesting couple, Michael Hannafin and Joan Scanlon, whose surnames are both "foreign". They had three children in the island, baptised in 1871, 1873 and 1875. Couples in which both parents were clearly outsiders are uncommon, particularly so late in the century. In only eight cases out of the more than 150 couples recorded in the baptismal register up to 1910 do both parents have non-island surnames.

The island surnames, of course, also occurred on the mainland, so that there may have been outsiders among the O'Sheas, Kearneys and so forth, but there can be no doubt about the non-island origins of the following couples (the date of the first baptismal entry is given in brackets): Sheehy/Bowler (1817); Kavan/Ferriter (1824); Fitzgerald/Kennedy (1825); Moore/Kavan (1830); Manning/Long (1830); Murphy/Doody (1833); O'Brien/Murphy (1838); Hannafin/Scanlon (1871). The early dates of all but the last couple links these families with the outward movement of population from mainland to island associated with the dramatic rise in the birthrate during the early nineteenth century.

*Island men going to Mass in Dunquin. Since there was no chapel on the Blasket,
islanders rowed to the mainland each Sunday.*

Michael "Buffer" Keane behind his house. The "Buffer", a brother of Pats-Vicky Keane, the "king" of the Blaskets, was a tough little man and one of the best fishermen on the islands. This photograph shows the salt stains all islanders got on their clothes from their life on the sea (circa 1930.)

4

The Blaskets during the Famine

Little news from the Blaskets is carried in the Kerry newspapers during the years of the Great Famine. The oral tradition, recorded by Tomás Ó Criomhthain, that no island people died of starvation may possibly be true, although the fall in the population from 153 people in 1841 to 97 in 1851 suggests otherwise. The population decline is, however, proportionately smaller than on the mainland, and recovery on the Blaskets was more rapid and complete. Another tradition held by the island people, that the blight never reached the island, cannot be wholly accepted, though there may have been partial immunity. Irish islands seem, on the whole, to have been less severely stricken by blight than the mainland. Newspaper reports during the 1850s when the blight, though decreasing, was still prevalent, indicate that the western seaboard of the Dingle peninsula was more susceptible to disease than other parts, especially inland areas of Kerry. The Blasket is specifically mentioned in 1857 as having the blight unusually early that year.

The natural food resources of the Great Blasket — fish, shell-fish, seaweeds, seabirds and their eggs, rabbits — must have been strained to their limits before the Famine by the expanding population of the 1830s. As mentioned above, the 1841 census recorded 153 inhabitants on the main island, which was at a later date estimated by one observer to be capable of supporting "perhaps a score of people".[13] There is no doubt about the poverty of the islanders at this time. Did they have some marginal advantage over the poor living on the nearby mainland where the death toll was so appallingly heavy? Dunquin parish, for example, lost almost half its population between 1841 and 1851.

Two external factors mitigated the distress experienced on the Great Blasket. One was the relief-work carried out during the 1840s by the Dingle and Ventry Mission Association. The other was a series of shipwrecks whose salvage helped the island people survive the years from 1850 onwards.

The Dingle and Ventry Mission, a Protestant organization, first established a foothold on the Great Blasket in 1839-40 when it opened the island's first school under a resident agent cum teacher cum Scripture reader. The proselytising activities of the Mission, both on the mainland and on the island are controversial. Nevertheless, it cannot be denied that during the Famine the Mission operated considerable relief schemes in Dingle and the remote western parishes, particularly during the early years of the emergency when official relief was barely organised and totally inadequate. It is doubtful if official relief supplies would have reached the Blasket at all. The Mission's own six-oared boat seems to have been almost the only contact between the island and the mainland during the years of stress. The Mission's work in Ventry, Dunquin and the Blasket was organized by the Reverend Thomas Moriarty, minister at Ventry, who was the prime founder of the Ventry Relief Committee which had been authorised by the Tralee Guardians in July 1847 to administer relief in the western parishes, areas which had until then been largely neglected by the Dingle Relief Committee.

Around 1846 or 1847 a boiler was installed in the Blasket school from which soup and Indian meal stirabout were served. This was served as breakfast for the children in attendance, and was regarded as a bribe, but it is clear that by 1847 Indian meal (supplied in part by the British Association) was being served to *all* the children of the island, of convert and Roman Catholic families alike. In February 1848 there were between fifty-two and fifty-six children attending the school. The Mission's annual report for the previous year noted that, "The inspector of the BA allows rations for 35 children — that is, 17½ lbs. of meal per day. Jordan [the agent] had gone on feeding them all, as during the past year, and had to draw on his own stocks for the purpose. I promised to pay him and to enable him to continue the feeding of all the children."[14]

It also appears that some adult islanders were kept alive by paid labour provided by the Mission, mainly on walling and "improving the landing place". The standard rate for the period was eight pence a day for men and four pence for women. Though a modest amount, it was enough to purchase basic rations from Jordan's "own stock". Moreover, this was at a time when money was rarely handled by subsistence farmers, and paid labour was almost non-existent except on erratic government-sponsored "famine roads". The annual accounts of the Mission for 1847 show over £160 spent on the Blasket: £80.16.0. for the Blasket Relief Fund, £10 on rent of land in the island (a "farm" for converts), and £73 on "part of expenses of Blasquett Mission". Further amounts were probably included under such general headings as teachers' salaries, seeds supplied to poor farmers, lime for piers, clothing, medical supplies and so forth. The Reverend Mr. Moriarty writes of the island people in 1848, "I know not how the poor people will weather out this (coming) year, when most of them are as badly off, if not more destitute than ever."[15]

Miss Fitzgerald, the first teacher on the Blaskets under the Irish Free State,
stands outside the school house with her class, circa 1930.

The number of converts (as many as ten families are claimed by the Mission) should be treated with caution, but there is no reason to question the importance of the relief work carried out on the Blasket during this crucial period. By 1848 Mission funds were exhausted, and an earnest appeal was made to England for generous contributions to enable relief to continue. Among the Blasket projects, Moriarty mentions the completion of the landing place, and "making a passage to the only well in the island which never dries. When the others are dried up they have to let a person down the cliff by a rope."[16] Possibly he was referring to *Tobar an Rinn an Chaisleáin* ("Castle Point Well"), the cliff well near the village to which there is now a path.

In 1850 a dramatic change took place in the fortunes of the Dingle and Ventry Mission on the Blasket. During that year, possibly in the summer, Moriarty baptised a child, and some of the ladies of the Mission spent a day on the island with cloth and sewing materials, cutting out clothes for the children. But by the end of the year, the Soupers' school and teacher's house were both in a state of disrepair, and the breakwater, completed only three years previously, was also in need of repairs.[17] Moriarty wrote that £10 would cover both, but the accounts for the following year show that, though £5 was spent on the breakwater, no funds were allocated to the school. In 1850 the total expenditure listed under Blasket had dropped to about £42 of which £30 was the agent's salary. No mention is made of the pupils. Jordan was still resident in the island in November 1850, but neither the teacher's house nor the school is shown on a map dated 1 August 1851.[18] All but one of the convert families quickly returned to their mother church and although Moriarty is listed in the Griffith Valuation of 1850-51 as lessor of nearly half the island's houses and tenant of the land which had formed the converts' "farm", Protestant influence had within ten years come to a decisive end.

It cannot be a coincidence that the end of Protestant influence came in 1850, the same year in which the first of several shipwrecks occurred — wrecks described by the islanders as "heaven-sent". "Mara mbeath an long so do bhualadh ní bheadh duine beo san Oileán, adeirladh na sean-daoine. Cloisinn-se go maith chailleach bhéal-dorais go minic 'á rá gurbh é Dia do chuir ameasc na mbochtán í." ("If it hadn't been for that shipwreck, nobody would have survived in the island, the old people used to say. I often heard with my own ears the old hag over the way saying that God himself sent that ship among the poor.")[19] These wrecks rescued the island people not merely from starvation, as they openly acknowledged, but also from reluctant dependance on Protestant charity, an episode which is still under a shadow in the folk-memory.

These wrecks, which became embodied in the island folklore,

Blasket women collecting "shore food" in the 1920s.

can all be checked in Tralee newspapers of the period. The palm-oil ship was wrecked on the northern coast of the Great Blasket in March or April 1850. The Italian brig Caroline, carrying wheat, ran aground on the White Strand on 19 November of the same year, and was later the subject of a coroner's inquest, and severe rebuke by the coroner to the local population of both island and mainland, mainly for their callous ill-treatment of the corpses.[20] Many of the ship's crew were drowned, but when nine came ashore on the island "naked and distracted", Jordan reports that "the people shut their doors against them, until Patt Carney took three of them, and William Shea three, and myself three."[21] The third wreck, a Glasgow schooner, struck on Oileán na nÓg in late December 1853 or early January 1854. On this occasion, thanks to punctilious guidance by the island people, the crew came safely ashore and were warmly tended and fed.[22] The change in attitude no doubt reflects the softening of the people's own lives during the intervening three years.

OVERALL POPULATION TRENDS
DURING THE GREAT FAMINE

Official census returns show that the population of the Blasket Islands dropped by 30 percent between 1841 and 1851, from 156 people (including three on Inishvickillaune) to 109 (including eight on Inishvickillaune and four on Inis na Bró). Though considerable, this decrease is less severe than that in most places on the nearby mainland. For instance, Dunquin parish (which included the Blaskets) suffered a fall of nearly 50 percent overall, from 1,394 people to 722. The number had fallen even further by 1861, leaving a total of only 617 people in Dunquin parish. The Blaskets accounted for 98 of these (three on Inishvickillaune). In other words, the population of the Blaskets which in 1841 had made up only 11 percent of the parish, formed 15 percent in 1851 and nearly 16 percent in 1861. Not only was the population decrease smaller in the islands, but recovery was also more rapid and complete. Dunquin parish as a whole never recovered its pre-Famine total, whereas the Blaskets rose steadily: 138 (1871), 148 (1881), 139 (1891), 151 (1901), and 160 (1911). (A rapid and final decline after the Great War ended in total evacuation in 1953.) The slight fluctuations in the later nineteenth century figures can be attributed to emigration.

What proportion of the 1841-51 fall was due to death rather than emigration is difficult to determine, since no precise figures of either were recorded. A similar pattern of a proportionately smaller fall in population and fuller recovery on the island than on the mainland is reflected in a comparison of the Blasket baptismal rate with that of the whole parish of Ferriter (comprising the parishes of Dunquin, Dunurlin,

Children on the Great Blasket in 1924.

Kilmalkedar, Kilquane and Marthin). The baptismal registers of this large, composite parish show a peak baptismal rate in the Blaskets during the years of 1835-44. This was a period of population expansion and movement both on the mainland and in the islands, and the baptism register includes a number of family names which were new in the Blaskets. In 1845 there is a sudden and marked fall in the island entries and those of the parish as a whole. After the Famine, the number of baptisms from the Blaskets account for a significantly higher proportion of parish totals than before.

Why did the Blaskets have a better rate of survival and recovery than the mainland? The influence of the Dingle and Ventry Mission during the 1840s and of the timely wrecks of 1850-54 has already been considered. If a basic, minimum food supply could be maintained (as it seems to have been by these two external agencies), the insularity of island life had certain advantages. Geographical isolation provided some protection during the epidemics of "famine fever", dysentery and cholera which accompanied the starvation of the 1840s. The islands also escaped the wholesale evictions or "clearances" of tenants which took place on the mainland. The actual number of mainland Irish in such clearances is disputed, but there is no doubt that such practices were common during the period, and that they increased the number of people who died or were forced to emigrate. (Clara Hussey threatened the islanders with eviction in 1838-9, and actual evictions of half the tenants were attempted by Sam Hussey in the late 1870s. The latter were less than totally effective. Tomás Ó Criomhthain's stories of the Land War suggest that the islanders usually triumphed over the bailiffs.)

The combined effect, then, of various factors discussed above, was a mitigation on the Great Blasket Island of the worst effects of the Great Famine. Nevertheless the drop in population by over a third, from 153 to 1841 to 97 in 1851, remains stark evidence of the terrible set-back in island life which occurred. It is not remembered in this way, but only because the disasters to human society on the neighbouring mainland were so much worse.

Blasket men on the White Strand, circa 1920.

Visitors arriving at the tiny Great Blasket Harbour in the 1960s.

5
The
Harbour

The tiny harbour of *an Inncoin* (or *Caladh an Oileáin*) is virtually invisible from the seaward side of the Great Blasket. A small natural cove which was partly sheltered by an off-shore rock has been improved over the years by the addition of a concrete breakwater which joins the rock to the mainland cliff, leaving a narrow entrance, not more than ten feet wide even at high tide, at the north side of the tiny pool.

Before the breakwater was built, the landing-place was especially hazardous due to the strong-pulling currents which scour the Sound. Boats were often in danger of being swept through the gap between the rock and the island cliff. Tomás Ó Criomhthain tells of one occasion when a Dunquin man in a canoe was carried out of the Blasket Harbour on a spring tide all the way across Dingle Bay and landed, miraculously unharmed, at Valencia. His family was holding a wake for him when he got home. According to Tomás, it was because of this, which he dates at some time after the turn of the century, that the breakwater was built. Records of the Congested Districts Board, however, show that the Blasket boatslip and breakwater were under construction in 1893 and completed before 1899, at a total cost of £383.[23]

An earlier attempt to build a breakwater had been made during the 1840s, that bitter decade when the western extremity of the Dingle Peninsula was ravaged not only by famine, but also by an acrimonious religious struggle resulting from a campaign by Protestant missionaries, with financial support from English and Scottish sympathisers, to win converts among the starving Roman Catholic poor. The backward, western areas of Ireland were the most susceptible to such proselytising campaigns, and, by a combination of circumstances, Dingle had the dubious distinction of being one of the most vigorous centres of such activity, through the work of the Dingle and Ventry Mission.

According to the Mission's own chronicler, Mrs. A. M. Thompson, an attempt to introduce a Protestant "Bible reader" into the Great Blasket was made in 1835. When the islanders threatened to throw him over the cliff, he was hastily withdrawn. By 1838, however, the island people had softened sufficiently to ask the Mission for an Irish teacher and school. After some difficulty in finding a site, a school house was built and opened on the island in 1840. During the worst years of the Famine a few island families became converts, but once the emergency was over most of them returned to their mother church. By 1850 the already dilapidated Protestant school ("the old monastery of the Soupers", as Tomás Ó Criomhthain calls it) was closed.

During the 1840s, the Dingle and Ventry Mission maintained contact with the island by means of the missionary boat, which brought in building materials, workmen, books and furniture, relief-meal for the school boilers, as well as ministers and "friends" (mainly Protestant gentry from Dingle and elsewhere). Mrs. Thompson was one of those who visited the Blaskets. As the wife of Lord Ventry's land agent, she had personally collected from "a few Irish friends in England" the money required to build the school and teacher's house and pay the teacher's stipend (about £30 per year). She has left a fascinating account of her own visit to the island soon after the opening of the school in 1840. Among other matters, she describes the difficulty of landing at:

> the almost inaccessible path over the cliff called, and indeed forming, their only landing place . . . I had not been in it before, landing being difficult for a female, as it is necessary to take advantage of the swell of the wave and leap on the rocks from the boat, which perhaps is the next moment carried yards back on the retiring wave. The reader may believe I did not wear anything very handsome on such an expedition.[24]

No doubt it was as much for its own convenience as for the benefit of the islanders that the Dingle and Ventry Mission built a breakwater to protect the landing place. Like the schoolhouse, this breakwater remained intact for only a few years. A report from the Reverend Thomas Moriarty, written in 1850, reads:

> I regret to say that part of our breakwater at the Island was blown down. Indeed I wonder how it was not all swept away. This is one of the most useful works we got done during the famine. It actually made the only entrance to the Island, and forms in a small way a refuge harbour for fishing boats kept out there in the storm. A few pounds would restore it, otherwise we might expect the whole to be destroyed next winter. The schoolhouse and agent's residence must also be repaired if we would preserve them and the breakwater.[25]

These repairs were apparently not completed. The 1850 Annual Report of the Irish Society of London, which sponsored the Dingle and Ventry Mission, shows neither school nor agent on the island. It seems likely that this breakwater was indeed completely swept away in the storms of the next winter or two.

A few years earlier, in 1847, Captain Francis Eager of Dingle, the

Islanders in a naomhóg around 1930.

local agent for Lloyds shipping insurance company, submitted a proposal to Lloyds and also to the British Admiralty outlining the advantages of building "a safety harbour at the Blasquets". This proposal was also warmly championed by Father John Casey, the parish priest of Ferriter. This extraordinary scheme called for the building of a wall or bank of pebbles as a breakwater right across the *Bealach Caol* ("Narrow Sound") which divides Inis na Bró from Inishvickillaune, a distance of about half a mile in what can be very rough water, driven by strong currents. It is true, as the two gentlemen pointed out, that the passage is relatively shallow. The Admiralty Chart shows it to be between seven and nine fathoms deep at the narrowest point (i.e., between 42 and 54 feet). Captain Eager and Father Casey stressed the ease with which the project could be carried out, "the distance being only 800 yards". "The intermediate waters are not very deep, and there are plenty of stones on the islands to fill them up. Still better would be a wooden breakwater . . . through whose openwork the incoming waves might pass and subside into calm." Perhaps as a particular inducement to the Admiralty they claimed that "the junction of the two islands would make a harbour safe and capacious enough for the British Fleet".[26] The whole scheme is pure fantasy. Anyone who has stood on Black Head at the western end of the Great Blasket Island and watched the tide racing through that narrow gap of "only 800 yards" will not be surprised that the report seems to have been quietly pigeon-holed by Lloyds and their Lordships of the Admiralty.

Whether the island people or the inhabitants of Dunquin would have welcomed the stationing of the British Fleet just outside their back door is questionable. Mike Peig Sayers, the island poet, tells of the panic caused in the Blasket village during the First World War (when Irishmen were liable to conscription into the British forces) by the sight of a British warship anchored to the north, her boat pulling for the island. All the youths of call-up age slipped hurriedly round the "Gob" (the island headland to the south of the harbour) in canoes to take refuge on Inishvickillaune until the warship had steamed away and was safely out of sight. Later it was discovered that the vessel had only called to take on fresh water.

The Blasket harbour, as restored by the Congested Districts Board, can accommodate only a few small boats at any one time, and they must be boats of shallow draught such as dinghies or keel-less canoes or currachs (the local name for this boat is *naomhóg*). Even then it was rare for these canoes to be left in the water for long. They were normally lifted out and laid, bottom up, on stays halfway up the cliff, or high up at the side of the slip out of reach of freak waves. Only one canoe can pull alongside the slip at a time, and low tide is avoided whenever possible. One of the surveys of the Congested Districts

Board, issued between 1892 and 1898, lists twelve canoes employing thirty-six men on the Great Blasket. The total population in 1891 was 132, living in twenty houses. By 1911, the population had risen to 160, with twenty-nine occupied houses. It is probable that there were several more canoes in use then. Old photographs show the track down to the harbour lined with canoes lashed down on stays and weighted against the wind with stones. At busy times, as when a shoal of mackerel or mass of floating wreckage was sighted, there must have been considerable congestion in the little harbour. There is no other landing place, unless, like the more daring of the island men, you trust yourself to leap straight out of a boat onto a cliff-ledge. The deceptively alluring White Strand, is dangerous, especially in winter, because of strong currents, although a map of the south coast of Ireland drawn up for the British Admiralty in the 1790s shows a safe anchorage "for the duration of one tide" just off its northern end.

This anchorage, off the end of White Strand, seems to correspond with the unidentified "Harbour of Vicey" in the Blasket Sound known to Juan Martinez de Recalde, Admiral of the Armada Fleet. His flagship, the 1,050 ton San Juan, along with another ship, the 750 ton San Juan Batista, successfully sheltered there from gales for six days in September 1588, although two other Armada ships were wrecked in the Sound within their sight. The journal of Marcos de Aramburo, paymaster and controller of the galleons of Castille, who was on the San Juan Batista, provides a graphic account of the experiences of this storm-tossed vessel. The ship's crew blindly followed Recalde "despairing of any remedy, and we ignorant of the coast". They doubled round one of the islands (probably Inis Tuaisceart) slipping through an entrance between low rocks "about as wide as the length of a ship". It is thought that somehow they negotiated the narrow passage between *Carraig Fhada* and the rocks to the north, identified on the Admiralty chart as Ballyclogher Rocks but known to the local people as *Bolg Lineach*. The distance is less than 100 yards. Recalde obviously knew what he was aiming for. He had previous acquaintance with this treacherous coast, having been commander of the fleet which landed the 600 Spanish troops who were savagely slaughtered by English soldiers at *Dún an Oir* in Smerwick Harbour in 1580. According to the Kerry curse, there were only five survivors from the massacre — "Marbhú an Dúna ort nár tháinig ach cúrgear slán as!" ("The death of the Doon on you, from which only five came out alive!")

Vicey, the name of the harbour into which Recalde guided Aramburo's ship, is not known to island people nor does the word bear any resemblance to any placename now known in the area. But it is clear from Aramburo's log that it was close to the Great Blasket. One islandman remembers his father showing him the only channel through which a big ship could safely pass between the Great Blasket and Beiginis. He indicated the exact route by lining up certain rocks off the north-east headland with one on *Carraig Fhada,* and then with one of the jags of *Barra Liath* on Inis Tuaisceart, thus demonstrating in reverse part of the route Recalde may have followed into the haven of Vicey.

It was on the White Strand that an Italian brig, the Caroline, was wrecked in November 1850. Her crew were all drowned. Less than four years later, in January 1854, a new Scottish cargo vessel (copper-bottomed and bolted) returning from Genoa to Glasgow, sprang a leak off Gibraltar and drifted, with her sails blown away, all the way up to Kerry. She finally drove on to *Oileán na nÓg* near Beiginis and sank. Her crew, six men and two boys, managed to take to the boat and pulled for the White Strand where they would have attempted to land if the islanders had not warned them off by making signs with their hats and walking along the cliffs directing them to the proper landing place. For as a local correspondent of the *Tralee Chronicle* wrote "no boat ever attempted to land there in this season of the year". When the exhausted crew finally did approach the landing place, the island people, both men and women, waded into the water up to their waists to help them out of the boat. Then they took them home, warmed, dried and fed them on what little they had, which was potatoes and fish.[27]

In calm weather and at certain states of the tide it was possible for a small boat to beach or put men ashore in some of the small coves of the northern headland. One is in fact called Boat Cove (*Cuas na mBád).* None of these coves, however, is easy to climb out of. Gravel Strand *(an Tráigh Gearaí)* had to have a trackway cut into the cliff (now partly collapsed) to enable sheep to be driven down to the strand for shearing.

The lack of any safe landing place on the island other than the harbour carried certain advantages. During the "Land War" and at other times when the islanders were being harried by landlords' agents, rent-collectors, tax-collectors, bailiffs and the like, it afforded a degree of protection. The village has a wide enough view of the mainland coast to allow fair warning of any approaching boat, and to afford time to prepare for the reception of unwelcome officials at the landing place. Tomás Ó Criomhthain's stories of livestock being driven to the far western end of the island before the bailiffs arrived to confiscate them, and of the island women bombarding bailiffs with boulders from the top of the harbour cliff are confirmed by Sam Hussey, one of the landlord's agents.[28] The reputation the islanders had acquired, whether well-founded or not, was also remarked on by J. M. Synge who recorded impressions of his visit to Ballyferriter and the Great Blasket Island in August 1904: "It is told in Ballyferriter that a landlord's bailiff went out to the Blaskets some half century ago and that they

The Great Blasket Island slip in 1962.

tied a stone round his neck and threw him into the sea."[29] The fact that the Earl of Cork's last rental list, submitted to the Congested Districts Board in 1907, shows that no one on the island had paid rent for at least eleven and a half years suggests that the islanders made intelligent and resourceful use of whatever geographical advantages they had. The awkwardness of the tiny harbour was a positive benefit to them at such times, and the lack of an alternative landing place gave them considerable security.

One story, however, told by Tomás Ó Criomhthain, shows that on at least one occasion the bailiffs evaded the islanders' vigilance.[30] They approached the island from the side, landing a small party at a point below the southern cliffs from which they climbed up and then stole down upon the village from the hill behind. Meanwhile their boat crept round the island towards the harbour under the shelter of the cliffs, ready to receive whatever booty the bailiffs could seize in lieu of rent. They were clever enough to choose a time when the men of the island were at sea, fishing. The spot where the bailiffs landed is not recorded in the story, and it is difficult to imagine where it could have been. Nevertheless, it must have been no easy place, which perhaps explains why the bailiffs when they finally reached the village and started the mean work of tearing the thatch off the poet Dunleavy's roof were so easily routed by the poet's spirited wife armed with her husband's sheep shears. This episode certainly pre-dates the building of the slip and breakwater by the Congested Districts Board in the 1890s, for the poet died an old man about 1890. Tomás's story also suggests that the poet's children were quite young at the time. The poet's wife, Mary Manning, was (according to Ó Criomhthain) unaware of the bailiff on the roof until a handful of thatch fell into the skillet in which she was preparing the children's dinner. The baptismal registers of the parish of Ferriter show that the Dunleavys had four children baptised between 1837 and 1850, so that, if our chronicler's details are authentic, this event can be assigned to a date not later than the 1860s.

Dunmore Head, Beiginis, and the eastern part of the Great Blasket, from 15,000 feet.

6

The Island Village and its Houses

Any permanent human settlement has certain basic requirements: shelter, fresh water and a means of subsistence. Shelter on an exposed Atlantic island can be only partial, but the butt-end of the mountain ridge which forms the Great Blasket gives some protection from the prevailing westerly winds. Additional shelter was gained by the islanders by half-burying their homes in the hillside, just as many of the ancient clocháns (beehive huts) found on the Great Blasket, Inis Tuaisceart, the slopes of Mount Eagle and elsewhere were bedded below ground level.[31]

Tomás Ó Criomhthain lists over twenty springs and wells on the Great Blasket. Several are found in the village, although some on the cliff face are not easily reached. The best, known variously as *Tobar Barra 'n Bhaile* or *Tobar a' Phúncáin,* is located at the top of the village and was uncovered towards the end of the last century. We have never known it to run dry, but normally it gives no more than a steady trickle. As a result it became a great place for conversation as people waited for their buckets to fill.

The sea, one main source of food, is never far away, but it is only easily accessible at the eastern end of the island where the few strands lie. Most of the island's cultivable land, a small area of comparatively low, level ground, is also at the eastern end of the island and lies adjacent to the village. So it would be hard to find an alternative site on the island for a permanent human community. The eastern end of the island also lies closest to the mainland, a matter not only of physical convenience but also of psychological importance. For, whatever their sense of independence and consciousness of being a separate community, the islanders were necessarily dependent on the mainland for trade and the services of doctor, priest, post and police.

The Blaskets lacked sufficient natural resources to be self-supporting. Such a tiny community — 176 is the highest population recorded (1916) — could not support a shop, public house or any regular supply service, let alone doctor, nurse or priest.[32] It did have a National School from about 1860 onwards with one, sometimes two, resident teachers. A post office with telephone was also instituted in the 1930s. Lying so close to the mainland may have reduced the incentive to build up internal services, even if that had been possible, for visits to Dingle and Dunquin, to shops and fairs, however time-consuming, laborious and often dangerous, were anticipated outings and social events.

Despite its proximity to the mainland, the Blasket was often cut off by bad weather for long periods, especially in winter. The sense of isolation people experience can be out of all proportion to the actual distance, and there is no doubt that a certain reassurance was derived from the lights of Dunquin and Coumenole across the Sound. Most island families were connected by blood or marriage with the mainland families, and although the relationship between island and mainland was somewhat ambivalent (involving bitter rivalries on the fishing-grounds, for instance), there was an emotional as well as an economic dependence on the mainland. Perhaps the final indication of this is the islanders' practice of returning to the mainland for burial. Though the priest had to be fetched from as far away as Ballyferriter, and the coffin and the necessities for the wake had to be brought from Dingle, and still another journey (amounting to three or four in all) had to be made for the interment, islanders always returned to the mainland for burial. The island had no proper graveyard, apart from a little *cealúrnach* where unbaptised infants, suicides and a few shipwrecked mariners were buried. A conversation between young Maurice Ó Sullivan, a recent arrival on the island, and his grandfather, quoted in *Twenty Years A-Growing,* reveals the islanders' attitude:

"And isn't it strange they wouldn't have a graveyard here for themselves? Upon my word, daddo, if I were dying I would order my body to be buried above at the tower."

"Musha, my heart, you would do no such thing. It would be another matter if others were buried there before you."[33]

It is significant that it was a delay in getting a coffin to the mainland in the early 1950s which finally made the island people decide to evacuate to the mainland.

The village as it now stands is a survival of an old type of mountain village, once common but now rarely found. The slope on the Blasket is uncomfortably steep, and exposed on three sides to strong winds and heavy rain. The remains of thirty-four or thirty-five houses and some outbuildings can be seen in various states of preservation. Most of them conform to the traditional type of Irish "cabin" — a long, single-storeyed building with walls of unmortared stone, built on a simple, rectangular ground plan, and divided internally into two rooms, kitchen and bedroom (*cistin* and *seomra*), by means of a wooden screen, with a loft at either end for storage and extra sleeping space. By tradition, houses on sloping sites were built at right angles to the contours, with the hearth-gable (here the west gable) bedded into

Tig na Gabha
A typical island cottage

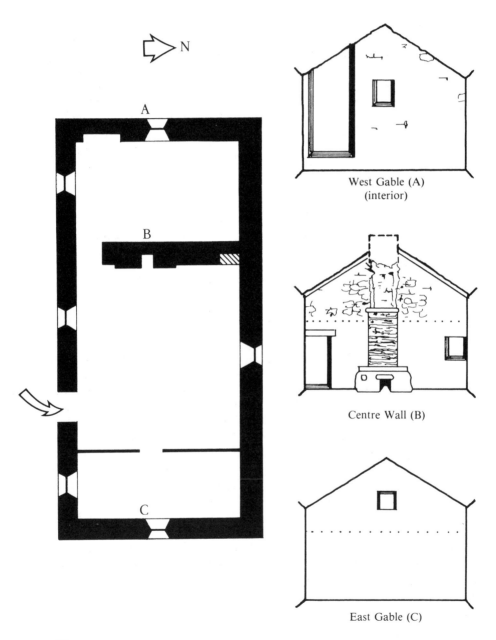

N

A

B

C

West Gable (A)
(interior)

Centre Wall (B)

East Gable (C)

the hillside. Two-thirds of the Blasket houses, all those built before 1910, lie along this west-east axis. The gradient, especially towards the top of the village, is so steep that some of the houses are more than half-buried on their west and north sides. Before building, a wedge-shaped excavation was made into the hillside to provide a level site. The steeper the slope, the bigger and deeper the wedge. The masonry of the west gable is actually bedded into the exposed earth face. The hearth and chimney helped counteract the inevitable damp of that wall, but larger houses built around the turn of the century often had a narrow bedroom behind the hearth. The rear (north) wall is not bedded in, but has a narrow gap between the wall and earth-face to provide a drainage channel. Roofs and chimneys of many houses barely rise above ground level at the back; hence the stories of animals and human invaders from above, and the drying of fish on the roof. Each house is tucked into its own niche, one above the other in random fashion, like sea-birds nesting on a cliff.

Measurements of the old cottages are given in the 1850 housing survey:

Tenant		Grade	Length ft. in.	Breadth ft. in.	Height ft. in.	Rateable Value
			—— W A L L S ——			
Daniel Crohan	house	3C	17 0	13 0	5 0	4s. 6d.
	office	3C	7 0	12 0	5 6	
Thomas Kearney	house	3C+	22 0	15 0	6 0	9s. 7d.

Walls were low and thick, windows small and deep-set. The houses were primarily bastions against the weather, and consequently were so dark that the door was left open whenever possible to let in some light. (Some houses had fitted half-doors.) The older houses have only one door located on the south face and centrally positioned with a window on either side; a tiny window high in the east gable lit the sleeping loft. Very few older houses have windows in the north wall; where they exist they seem to be later additions. Tomás Ó Criomhthain's childhood home is the only one recorded having a north door. It faced the house of Tomás "Maol" Ó Ceárna ("Bald" Tom Kearney) and was so close that either housewife could have scalded the other from her own doorstep.[34] These two houses were almost certainly the survivors of two short parallel rows of houses shown on the 6-inch Ordnance Survey map of 1840 near *Rinn an Chaisleáin*. The group has a curious foreign look since straight terraces or streets are not normal here. Nothing is known of their origin and they are not shown on the second edition of the 6 inch map in 1895. Tomás moved into his own large, new house, nearby, in 1892. Tomás Ó Criomhthain's new three-roomed house measures 37 feet 6 inches by 16 feet 6 inches, with a shed roughly 6 feet by 12 feet. The height of the walls is now difficult to determine. It is typical of the better, larger type of house erected during a period of re-building during the 1890s, made possible by a decade of comparative prosperity in the fishing industry.

A few of the older houses show signs of alteration. The addition of rear windows, enlarged windows, an extra room on the back (giving a T-shaped ground plan), bear witness to the increasing demand for tourist accommodation during the present century.

There were no professional builders or masons on the Blaskets. Every man had to be his own builder, carpenter, glazier and jack-of-all-trades, with assistance and advice from relatives and neighbours. Skills were learned by imitation and measurements were judged by eye, nurturing conservatism in style and proportion. Whatever the size of the house, certain proportions remain constant. The pitch of the roof, and the rise of the roof, which was always roughly identical with the height of the front wall, resulted in the frontage being bisected longitudinally, half black, half white, a most pleasing effect. Internally, all the rooms occupy the full width of the house. The kitchen is always the largest room, the bedroom and the back room (if any) are always narrow, rarely more than 8 feet across, just wide enough to wedge a bed in crosswise at one end. Even today, in some mainland houses, the fit is so tight one feels that the beds must have been installed before the partition wall was built.

The layout of the furniture was standardized to a large extent, with the dresser invariably along the boarded partition facing the hearth, to the left of the bedroom door. This position derives from the use of the dresser as a room-divider in the old one-roomed cottages, particularly important as the bed was usually sited behind it. The table stood against one of the long walls usually under the window, with the bench or "settle" against the other.

Pegs in the walls held a paraffin lamp and pictures; the mirror was normally hung by the door for light.[35] Materials for building were what lay at hand — stone, mud, reeds for thatching, and driftwood. By the end of the nineteenth century increasing fishing trade enabled some materials to be bought in Dingle. There is no shortage of stone in the Blaskets, but there are no trees; hence the persistence here, and on the nearby mainland, of the corbelled beehive hut (clochán) which needs no timber to support its roof. Relics of ancient clocháns lie towards the western end of the island. The fine example standing intact in the village is no more than a century old and was built as an outbuilding, not a dwelling. There are no obvious remains of dwelling houses of this type in the village, and it may be inferred from the pointedness of the references to the clochán on Inis Tuaisceart which was inhabited during

*The sole clochán (right) in the village was constructed about
100 years ago as an outbuilding.*

Map 5
The Village - Great Blasket Island
(Not to Scale)

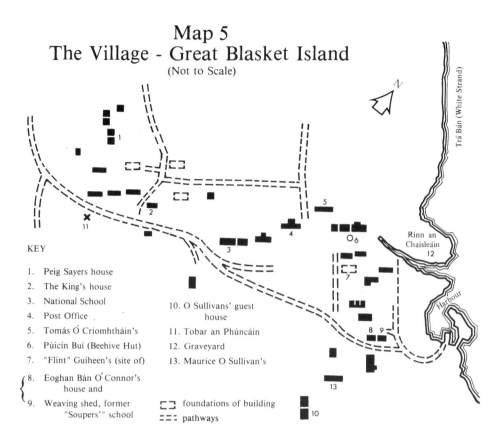

KEY

1. Peig Sayers house
2. The King's house
3. National School
4. Post Office
5. Tomás Ó Criomhtháin's
6. Púicín Buí (Beehive Hut)
7. "Flint" Guiheen's (site of)
8. Eoghan Bán Ó Connor's house and
9. Weaving shed, former "Soupers'" school

10. O Sullivans' guest house
11. Tobar an Phúncáin
12. Graveyard
13. Maurice O Sullivan's

▭ foundations of building
═══ pathways

Trá Bán (White Strand)

Rinn an Chaisleáin 12

Harbour

the 1830s that this was an abnormal practice, at least at that date. Driftwood timbers must have been used to support the thatch of the small rectangular cottages of the 1850s. Tarred felt began to replace thatch during the re-building period of the 1890s, though one thatch survived until 1940.[36]

The masonry was uncoursed, roughly shaped or untooled stone. It was mortared with mud or clay, often with large boulders incorporated in the base. There is no quarry of any size on the Blaskets, though the site of a small one can be found at the foot of the Gob, beyond the southern end of the village. Use was made of stones cleared from the fields, those excavated in house site preparation, from small pits, and from exposed faces and earth slips. During the constant fluctuations of population, masonry and timber from abandoned buildings was also used and re-used.

Door and window reveals, fireplaces and other openings requiring a straight edge were often lined with horizontal slivers of slate laid in close layers. Similar small masonry was used in the older houses to fill in the front of the chimney breast; this small masonry was not keyed in and was liable to fall out wholesale. For this reason the chimney breast was often covered with layers of tar and newspaper. Floors were of beaten mud or clay, reinforced at points of wear with inset stones or driftwood boards. The old hearths show an interesting combination of materials: irregular stone slabs and driftwood timbers bedded in with the intervening spaces filled in with "pitched" pebbles — thin sea pebbles set edge-wise into the floor, forming a miniature *chevaux-de-frise* which must have been acutely uncomfortable to the bare-footed girls and children. Whole floors of pitched pebbles, often set in decorative patterns, have also been found in Welsh cottages.[37] The pebbles in Blasket houses are set parallel, but there is no attempt at pattern and the areas are quite small. It was customary to scatter white sand over the hearth to soak up spills. In the old, dark houses with dark floors and blackened iron pots, it may also have helped the housewife to see what she was doing.

The first boarded floors used in the island were probably those in the Protestant school and teacher's house built about 1840, which later became the home of the O'Connor family. It is clear from the housing survey of 1850 that this house with its high walls and spacious proportions set a new standard in the village upon which island people later modelled their own houses during the period of re-building which started in the 1890s, a period of relative prosperity in the local fishing industry which was partly stimulated by the new harbours at the Blasket and Dunquin and by the new Dingle-Tralee Railway. Tomás Ó Criomhthain's new house built during this decade is almost three times the size of the old one, with a tarred roof and other new features including an iron plate let into the chimney breast to replace the older timber crane. Such developments were typical of a number of houses built during the next ten to fifteen years.

Most of the eighteen houses surveyed in 1850 were small, some very small, and of a poor standard. None has survived in its original state; many were pulled down or enlarged after 1890. A local government official reported in 1886 that the islanders seemed "pretty well off" but that their houses were "wretched".[38] When the Congested Districts Board took over the island in 1907, it condémned and eventually replaced six houses as unfit and "improved" another.[39] The Board's first plan was to build five and improve one, but in their final account in 1917 distinctive purchase prices were charged to seven tenants. It seemed that some time between 1907 and 1917 the Board agreed to sponsor an additional new house, which was built for an island family in the lower village by a builder from Ballyferriter. The new houses were under construction in 1910, and this date marks a turning-point in housing style in the Blasket, literally as well as figuratively, since every house from that time onwards faced east instead of south.

The poor standard of housing in Ireland had been a constant subject for comment by travellers since Elizabethan times. Sporadic attempts to raise the standard had been taken by a few "improving" landlords on their own estates during the late eighteenth and the nineteenth centuries, but well-meant improvements did not always accord with the immediate needs of the tenants. Arthur Young reported cases of tenants moved out of wretched windowless and chimneyless hovels and then stopping up the windows and chimneys of their new cottages, presumably to keep the warmth in.[40] Remote impoverished rural areas continued to be neglected. Landlords were not responsible for providing houses; normally the tenant erected his own. It is worth noting that, in the Griffith Survey of 1850, out of a total of £63, the land on the Blasket was valued at £56.11.0. and the buildings at a mere £6.9.0. The Protestant teacher's house was assessed at £1 and the school house at 18s., whereas the islanders' seventeen houses together totalled only £4.11.0., an average of just under 5s. 6d. each.[41] By 1907 the valuation had changed little: the land was valued at £53.15.0. and the buildings (twenty houses) at £7.0.0. There is no evidence that the landlord or his agents ever erected any houses on the Blaskets, except for the ill-fated "milk house" on Beiginis — a large, solid stone building erected early in the nineteenth century and derelict by 1856.

Rural housing needs had been one of the subjects of recommendation by the Devon Commission Report in the 1840s, but it was not until the end of the century that the provision of adequate rural housing was accepted as a matter of government responsibility. Between 1883 and 1906 various Local Government Board for Ireland (Labourers) Acts laid down minimum specifications for housing, including recommendations for damp courses and air-bricks and a number of optional concessions to Irish rural life such as iron fire cranes and stone chopping blocks for firewood. Designs for model labourers' cottages were published. The Congested Districts Board had eight standard designs for four-roomed dwelling houses, five of which were single-storeyed, reflecting the traditional preference for this type of home. Estimated costs of each design are given, varying between £145 and £151 at 1914 prices. It is interesting to note that labour costs amounted to less than one third of the total, using skilled masons, carpenters, plasterers and slaters, with (wherever possible) local unskilled labourers.[42] Many of the islandmen were employed as building labourers on the houses erected by the Congested Districts Board on the Great Blasket; this was part of the Board's educative function, as well as an economy and form of public relief.[43]

It is not clear why, early in the twentieth century, the Board decided on two-storeyed houses for the Blasket in defiance not only of local tradition but also of local climatic conditions. Instead of cowering

Traditional 19th century island houses facing south.

*House designed by The Congested Districts Board and built in the early
20th century face east.*

into hollows, the five of new houses (two pairs semi-detached, one detached) stand up into the wind on an exposed site at the top of the village, with doors back and front and large windows on all faces. The semi-detached idea was also new in the island and on the Dingle Peninsula generally. (The Devon Commission's quaint warning against the evils of the "double cottage" need not be taken too seriously. "Of all the ingenious contrivances for creating and maintaining discord, nothing can compare with the double cottage. War is the result . . . a war of words, of women, of cocks, dogs, pigs and children . . . with missiles of attack ever at hand, stones, brooms, boiling water, and that most venomous weapon of all, the uncontrolled tongue . . .[44]) In almost every way these houses were foreign to the local style. The materials used were new: concrete and slate, with a large quantity of timber used for the staircase and floors. J. M. Synge reported "one or two roofs of slate" before this, in 1905, but we have not been able to identify them. A sketch (highly inaccurate in other respects) of the Protestant school about 1840 also shows what appears to be a slate roof.[45] Tomás Ó Criomhthain reported that the school and teacher's house fell into disrepair soon after the Famine. They were later taken over as a dwelling house and weaving-shed by the O'Connor family. These houses are now roofless, but there are no quantities of slate among the debris. Their height and the fact that they are built along the contours on a north-south alignment, make them conspicuous, though there was some attempt to fit into the local pattern by siting them in a staggered line and by keeping the upstairs windows to the sides and back, so that the upper storey is disguised from the front.

The north-south alignment was the only new feature of the Board's houses which was adopted by all the subsequent island builders. It is interesting to observe how much each builder adopted the new ideas and materials, while assimilating them into the traditional style and scaling them down to the old proportions. Two houses (Eoghan's and Caisht's) built before 1920 are virtually traditional houses, except that they are swung round 90 degrees. Another house (O'Sullivan's), built before 1917, very successfully combines many modern features — large windows, front and rear doors, slate roof, an extensive range of outbuildings at the rear — with traditional proportions. Only the last two houses, built in the 1930s, were double-storeyed. One (built originally as an extension) copies the Board's houses in keeping the upstairs windows to the sides and back; the height is scaled down, and, with traditional masonry and tarred felt roof, it is perfectly in harmony with its neighbours. The other, modelled on a mainland type, was designed as a guest house and is conspicuously different from the dwelling houses. This was the last house to be built, in 1936, and is to be found at the extreme southern end of the village.

The newer, east-facing houses lie on the fringes of the old village. One reason the old village did not extend to the south of the harbour seems to have been that this area *(an Gort Bhán)* was retained by the Crown for defence purposes until 1839. It was then leased to the Dingle and Ventry Missionary Society at the "exorbitant" rent of £5 per annum.

The island village while still inhabited in the 1930s.

House of Eoghan Bhán O'Connor, the Weaver

(Originally the Dingle and Ventry Mission School).

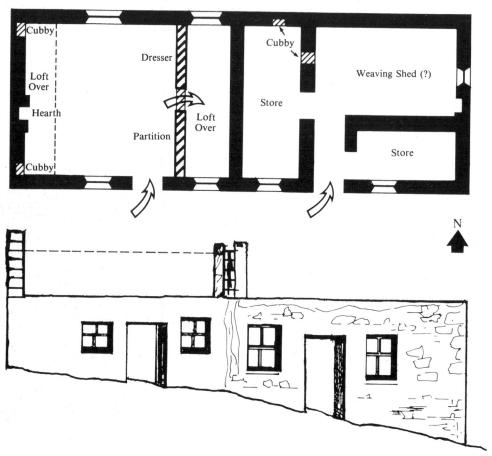

Mary Keane and Kate Keane with the Celtic scholar Robin Flower in an island house.

The Great Blasket island village and fields, from the sea.

7

The Development of the Field System

In 1907 the Great Blasket was purchased from the Earl of Cork's estate by the Congested Districts Board, which then spent ten years re-organising the system of land-tenure and building several new houses. Up to that time, as we know from Robin Flower, the islanders had held their arable land under the old rundale system, whereby each tenant's cultivated land was scattered in small, separate unfenced strips over an area of large open fields similar to the medieval open field system of English villages.

Despite their relatively recent disappearance from the Blasket, very little is remembered of the rundale strips and open fields, and still less is recorded of their position and layout. Tomás Ó Criomhthain lists the names of twenty cultivated fields: *Gort na gCearc, an Gort Bán, an Trasnán, Cúil an Chamaraigh, An Gort Fada, An Slinneán Bán, Tobar an Phúca, Ceann an Ghuirt, an Gainimh, Port an Eidhneáin, an Fearann Gearra, Gort an Áird, an Fhothrach, an Gort Nuadh, an Seana-Ghort, Garrdha Gála, Béal na Trágha, an Trasnaigh, Idir-Dhá-Chasán* and *an Duimhe* (in three sections: *an Duimhe Bhocht, an Duimhe Mhór* and *an Duimhe Mhór Bán*). He does not give any indication of their position or of their relation (if any) to the present field layout. Since there are now eighty fields, it is clear that Ó Criomhthain must be referring to some layout prior to the Board's re-organisation.

It was not until 1974 when, with the help of one of the island families, we were collecting the names of the present-day fields, that we discovered that a number of fields carried identical names. There were, for instance, ten with the name *Garraí Gála*, and sixteen called *an Duimhe*, each differentiated by the addition of the owner's name — *Duimhe an Phúncáin, Duimhe Pheats Shéamuis* and *Garraí Gála Sheáin Uí Shé*. The synonymous fields in each group proved to be contiguous and once they were blocked in on paper, each group produced the outlines of twenty-one larger fields. Five were very large: *an Duimhe* (includes sixteen modern fields); *Garraí Gála* (ten); *an Slinneán Bán* (eight); *Tobar an Phúca* (seven), and *an Gort Fada* (four). Ten were smaller: *an Trasnán* (three); *an Talamh Garbh* (three); *an Trasnaig* (three); *an Fearann Gearra* (two); *Ceann an Ghoirt* (three); *Cúil an*

Fhothrach (two). Four names occurred singly: *an Ghainimh, Port an Eidhneáin, an Seana-Gort, Toibreacha an Lín,* and two separate, wedge-shaped fields which filled in awkward corners on the hill, both called *an Chúlóg.*

Three of the names given by Ó Criomhthain are missing from the map of the cultivated land allocated by the Congested Districts Board — *Gort na gCearc* and *an Gort Bán,* which lie on the opposite side of the village, and *Idir-Dhá-Chasán,* which seems to be an alternative name for the triangular field in *Garraí Gála.* Three of the names given to me in 1974 are not listed by Ó Criomhthain (the two *Cúlóga* and *Toibreacha an Lín*), and he lists *an Talamh Garbh* as "common", not arable land. Otherwise the names are identical. All the composite fields are listed by him as single fields, and despite many sub-divisions, their original boundaries stand so clear and uncompromised, both on the map and on the ground, that we seem to have stepped back in one stride seventy years, to the layout of the Blasket fields as they were before the Congested Districts Board's re-organisation began in 1907.

The first and second editions of the six-inch Ordnance Survey maps which are based on surveys made in 1840-41 and 1895 respectively, reveal some interesting developments in the field system during the sixty-six years between the first Ordnance Survey and the Congested Districts Board take-over. It is possible to plot the general outline of the land-tenure system in the island from 1841 onwards.

The first thing that strikes one about the 1841 map of the Great Blasket is its emptiness, not only in comparison with later maps of the island but also with the 1841 maps of the nearby mainland which, apart from the mountain areas, is shown to be much fragmented into small, sometimes tiny fields. The cultivated area at the north-eastern end of the Blasket is shown divided into eight sections, of which three together with a small part of a fourth correspond to the area of the arable land re-distributed by the Congested Districts Board. The other areas were treated by the Board mainly as pasture or outfield to be shared by several families, or as commonage. The westernmost area "H" (see Map 9, page 88) is edged by a line indicating an old ditch known as *Claointín* which can still be seen cutting straight across the backbone of the island from cliff to cliff, though it is not marked on any subsequent map. Its function is not clear; the area consists of rough mountain land, ranging between 500 and 600 feet high, and located on the very steep slope which rises to the ditch from behind the village.

Areas A, B and C on the map were, without doubt, the primary open fields of the rundale system in more or less their original form. Their outlines correspond precisely with boundaries shown on later field maps and with the field walls still in use today. It is impossible to judge exactly how old these primary fields are, for it is not yet

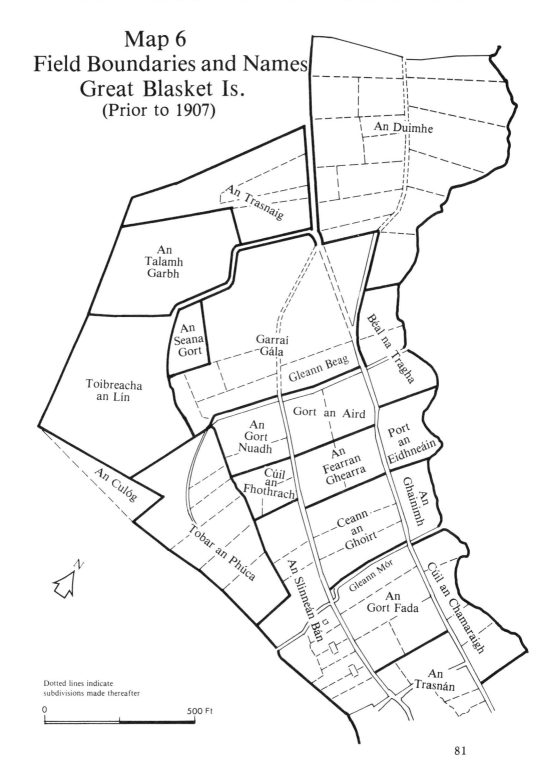

Map 6
Field Boundaries and Names
Great Blasket Is.
(Prior to 1907)

An Duimhe

An Trasnaig

An Talamh Garbh

An Seana Gort

Garraí Gála

Toibreacha an Lín

Gleann Beag

Béal na Tragha

Gort an Aird

An Gort Nuadh

An Fearran Ghearra

Port an Eidhneáin

Cúil an Fhothrach

An Ghainimh

An Culóg

Ceann an Ghoirt

Tobar an Phúca

Gleann Mór

An Slinneán Bán

An Gort Fada

Cúil an Chamaraigh

An Trasnán

Dotted lines indicate
subdivisions made thereafter

0   500 Ft

known how long the village site was inhabited. There are traditions, but no obvious remains, of an ancient church and castle here, but documentary evidence of any regular settlement is scanty. In September 1588 one of the Armada ships anchored in the Blasket Sound was reported as having sent a boat to the island every day "to refreshe themselves and to take water". There is no mention of inhabitants on the island. The first reference we are aware of does not occur until 1736, when the Sixth Earl of Orrery, who owned the Blasket at the time, saw from the mainland "some tillage and a few cabins". However, an earlier date of settlement may be inferred from Charles Smith's allusion to the island people's reputation for longevity in his *Ancient and Present State of the County of Kerry,* published in 1756, in which he says that no one had died on the island in the forty years before his visit. This takes us back, by implication, to the late seventeenth century at least. The great open fields and their boundaries which enclose most of the subsequent field developments may therefore be assumed to be at least three centuries old. Their names are not recorded. The oldest surviving names, such as *an Duimhe* and *Garraí Gála,* must date from the first stage of sub-division.

The boundaries which separate the three great fields from each other are in fact the channels of the two streams, *an Gleann Mór* and *an Gleann Beag,* which run from the upper boundary of the fields in parallel lines straight down to the sea. Their flow is seasonal, since they are fed by surface drainage from the marshy slopes plus occasional flood water from the hill. In summer they are normally dry. Their fall from about 300 feet to sea level is so short that both, particularly *an Gleann Mór,* have formed deep-cut channels which are difficult to cross even when dry. They thus pre-determined the boundaries of the three primary fields from west to east, that is, down the slope. A more rational division would seem to be from north to south or along the contours. One result of the west-east division was that each of these great fields extended across three levels and therefore three qualities of land, whereas a division along the contours would have given three more homogeneous areas — two fields of arable land, of slightly different qualities, and one of upland pasture and meadow. The upper levels of the Blasket fields are wet, tending to acidity. The lowest levels fringing the cliffs have dry, sandy soil. One field appropriately named *an Ghainimh* ("sandy place") is almost pure sand and now severely eroded. Between lies the most fertile areas of sandy loam. Both the middle and the lower levels have been consistently cultivated, mainly with potatoes and oats. It seems unlikely that the upper levels were ever substantially cultivated; they were probably used as pasture or meadow except during periods of extreme population pressure. Although the Great Blasket contains 1,132 acres, the cultivated area

The village and fields on the Great Blasket in the 1930s.

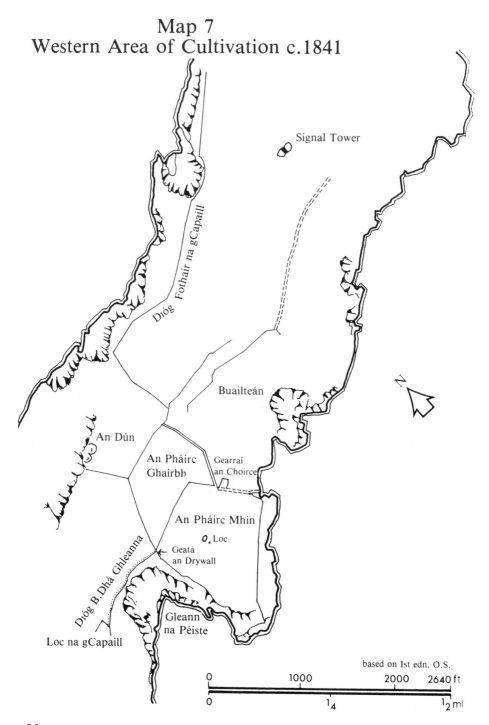

Map 7
Western Area of Cultivation c.1841

Signal Tower

Díóg Fothair na gCapaill

Buailteán

N

An Dún

An Pháirc Ghairbh

Gearraí an Choirce

An Pháirc Mhín

○ Loc

Geata an Drywall

Díóg B.Dhá Ghleanna

Loc na gCapaill

Gleann na Péiste

based on Ist edn. O.S.

0   1000   2000   2640 ft

0   ¹4   ¹2 ml

near the village amounts to not more than sixty-two or sixty-three acres, roughly one eighteenth of the total.

There is evidence of cultivation further back on the island. The 1841 map shows several large fields on the southern slope of the island above *Gleann na Péiste*. They can still be found and their names are known: *an Pháirc Mhín* or *an Pháirc, an Pháirc Gharbh,* and *Buailteán* (see Map 7). People now living remember driving the cows back daily to graze in this area where, among the rough mountain vegetation, there were expanses of fine smooth grass. Near the bottom of *Buailteán* is a small stone-walled enclosure known as *Garraí an Choirce* ("the Oat Garden") in which there are distinct cultivation ridges from six to seven feet wide which the islandmen identify as oat ridges. Ó Criomhthain refers to potatoes being grown here during his uncle's lifetime. This is the only enclosure shown on the 1841 map, but there is at least one other small patch of former tillage which can be observed nearby. *Garraí an Choirce* is not shown on the second edition of the Ordnance Survey map (1895). In the middle of *an Pháirc* is a sheep fold, *an Loc Dearg,* still identifiable. Leading down to *Garraí an Choirce,* the 1841 map shows a walled road, the only double-fenced road shown anywhere on the island at this time, which indicates a place of some importance.

Major walls or ditches are shown pushing westward from the village for about half the length of the island, as far as the Dun fort on the north and *Lac na gCapaill* ("Horses' Pound") on the south. Most of those with a *díog* (ditch) to their name such as *Díog na Leacan* and *Díog Fothair na gCapaill* have extensive protective ditches running along or parallel with the cliffs. Most of them seem to serve a triple function as fence, footway, and drainage channel. They connect the area of cultivation near the village to this second one near *an Pháirc.* Two of them, *Díog na Leacan* and *Díog Bharraan Dá Ghleanna,* have at various times been levelled and improved by Kerry County Council or Board of Works engineers and raised to the status of roadways. *Díog Bharraan Dá Ghleanna* is actually shown on the 1841 map as a boundary wall with a trackway. The 1895 edition shows it only as a boundary.

No house is shown near *an Pháirc* in the early Blasket maps. Very fragmentary remains of several clocháns lie close by but they are not indicated on the map either. It is possible that one or two families might have lived in the clocháns in the early nineteenth century, either all year round as on Inis Tuisceart or during the summer when "booleying". So far, no records of this place have come to light. We know only what Tomás Ó Criomhthain was told by the poet, Seán Ó Duinnshléibhe: namely, that he had heard from the old people of the island that there were six plough teams working on this slope, each

Map 8
Holdings of two tenants under the Congested Districts Board in 1917
(Dotted lines indicate sections of strand)

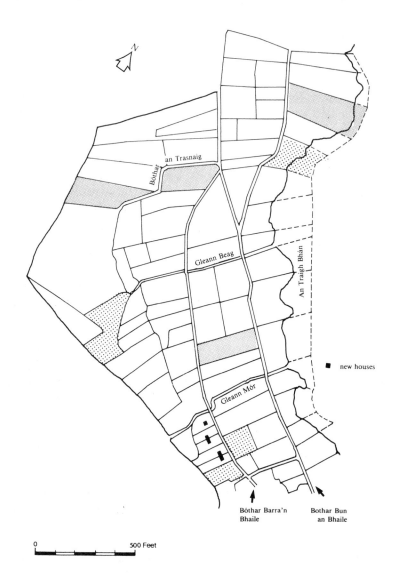

out of sight of the other. But this must be an exaggeration. What we see from the 1841 map is that this area was extensive, and that considerable use had been made of it before that date. This is consistent with evidence that population pressures and land hunger were driving families from the Great Blasket to colonise the outlying islands of the Blasket group during the first forty years of the nineteenth century, indeed as early as 1808. The population of the Great Blasket as recorded in the census of 1841 was 153, living in eighteen houses. Very little change is recorded between the first Ordnance Survey of 1841 and the second of 1895.

On the eastern, inhabited end of the island striking changes in cultivation patterns took place between 1841 and 1895. The great fields shown in 1895 are traversed by two access-roads from the village, *Bóthar Barraan Bhaile* and *Bóthar Bun an Bhaile,* running parallel to each other in a northerly direction and cutting each of the three main fields into three sections which roughly correspond to the three levels of land, with the result that the three soil types were now separated. A considerable amount of enclosure into smallish fields had taken place on the higher levels above the upper road. This undoubtedly represents individual tenure. The more fertile central area remains completely open, free from enclosure except for two small ones of curious shape. The lower sandy level also remains open except at the farthest northeast headland. It seems that a movement towards enclosure and consolidation of holdings had taken place on the marginal lands, on pasture and meadow land, but had barely touched the more valuable arable land (see Maps 8 and 10).

It is difficult to determine exactly when the access roads were laid down between 1841 and 1895. The winding *Bóthar an Trasnaigh* may be older than *Bóthar Barra an Bhaile* and *Bóthar Bun an Bhaile*. The curving outline of *Garraí Gála* which it follows is one of the primary boundaries found on the 1841 map, although it is not shown specifically as a road.

Comparison of the 1895 map with the map based on field names which can be approximately dated 1906 shows that the first subdivision of the middle and lower levels of the arable land must have taken place within that short space of ten or eleven years. *An Trasnán, Ceann an Ghoirt, an Fearran Gearra* and *Gort an Aird* in the middle area, and *an Ghainimh, Port an Eidhneáin* and *Béal na Trá* in the clifftop area were, therefore, comparatively new fields when the Congested Districts Board moved in. The number of unfinished walls shown on the 1895 map indicates perhaps that these fields were actually in the process of being enclosed when the survey was carried out.

The Earl of Cork's last rental roll, dated 1906, lists twenty

Map 9
Field Boundaries c.1841

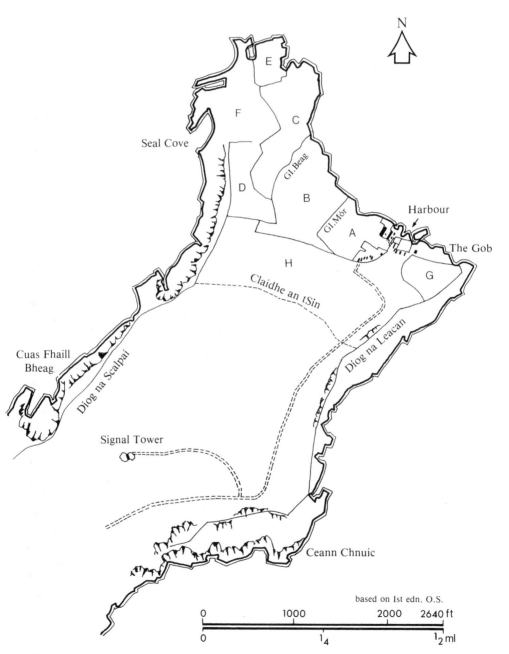

N

E

F

C

Seal Cove

Gl.Beag

D

B

Gl.Mór

A

Harbour

The Gob

H

Claidhe an tSin

G

Cuas Fhaill
Bheag

Diog na Scalpai

Diog na Leacan

Signal Tower

Ceann Chnuic

based on Ist edn. O.S.

| 0 | | 1000 | | 2000 | 2640 ft |

| 0 | | 1⁄4 | | 1⁄2 ml |

tenants, but this was undoubtedly out-of-date since no rent had been collected for seven and a half years. The census returns show twenty-one houses (one unoccupied) in 1891, but twenty-five in 1901. The total annual rent for the island was £40. The land was valued at £33 per annum, the houses and outbuildings at a mere £7. According to the accounts, the arrears of rent in 1906 amounted to £558. The purchase price paid by the Congested Districts Board in 1907 was £500. By the time the Board had completed its programme in 1917, there were thirty-one families in the Blasket. Of these, six were outside the Board's redistribution of land — three as sub-tenants, two as free-holders and one as "squatter". There were therefore twenty-five tenants among whom the Board had to re-allocate the land.

The arable land was not shared out equally among the twenty-five main tenants. The acreage allotted varied from nearly four acres to less than three-quarters of an acre. The criteria used are not clear. It might be assumed that the size of the new holding would correspond with the old but, assuming that the old annual rent of £1 to £4 per annum represented the amount of land held (less 7/- for the house) this does not seem to have happened. Nine tenants who previously paid £2 annual rent under the Earl of Cork were each allotted different size plots — four received three acres, three got two acres and the remaining two received just over one acre under the new dispensation.

Examination of the Board's map of the new holdings, dated 1917, shows two interesting features. First, the Board's layout of the fields kept entirely within the field boundaries already in existence. The outline of the cultivated area near the village remains precisely the same as it was in 1895 and 1841 with the addition of one wall only, yielding the narrow triangular *Culóg* ("back part") at the top of *Toibreacha an Lín*. Not a single field wall was removed or altered. New fields were created by sub-division of the existing fields into neat squares and rectangles, thus completing a process of sub-division started in 1841 which retained the boundaries of the primary open fields of the rundale system. Secondly, the Board retained the principle of scattered holdings. Governments, improving landlords and agricultural reformers since the eighteenth century had deplored the waste of time, labour and land involved in the primitive scattered strips of the rundale system and had advocated conversion to consolidated holdings. Yet, here on the Blasket, far from concentrating each holding into a block of adjacent fields, the Board allocated each tenant a number of fields scattered over the terrain in much the same way as the old rundale strips had been scattered. The size of the basic unit was larger but the principle was unchanged. This was not just a concession to island conservatism, but rather an attempt to ensure a fair distribution of good and less good land. Map 8 on page 86 shows fields allocated to two of the larger tenants. (These fields do not constitute the whole of their holdings. Both had shares in other fields outside the range of this map.) It will be seen that both holdings span almost the complete range of contours from the top ridge down to and including the sea-shore. This interesting compromise between ancient and modern was no doubt an inevitable consequent of the small amount of land available, and it is difficult to see how a more equitable system could have been devised. It is a fair gauge of its success that, after the upheaval of the change-over, the island people quickly recognised the advantages of their new fields and today speak of them as though they were the heritage of centuries.

Every holding included a section of strand, necessarily small since the Blasket has few beaches. The remainder of the island (about 1,070 acres) was divided into fifteen areas of commonage, held in equal shares by the twenty-five land-holders. Four marginal fields were shared in varying proportions among three groups of families. In *Toibreacha an Lín* rights of "undivided commonage" were shared among nine families in proportions ranging from one-twentieth to four-twentieths each. Two other fields were each shared by two families (the same two in each case). A fourth field was shared by two other families in the proportion of two to one. Each of these thirteen families also had a one-twenty-fifth share in the rest of the common land and were thus more advantaged than the remaining twelve commoners. Six families, the free-holders and sub-tenants, had no rights of commonage at all, unless by private arrangement, facilitated, as time went on, by vacancies left by emigration.

The common land was used mainly for grazing and turf-cutting. Anyone could cut the surface scraw-turf anywhere on the hill, but each commoner had his own area of rich black turf where no one else could dig. The best turf diggings were on *Sliabh Bharra an Dá Ghleanna* going westwards as far as *an Cró Beag* on the south side, and below and to the west of the *Dún* on the north side of the island. There was plenty of good turf even further west, but it made too long a journey for the donkeys. There were no carts on the Blaskets; the turf had to be carried in creels. There were also diggings on the hill north-west of the Signal Tower, made more accessible by the new road *(an Bhóthar Nua)* constructed in the 1930s to replace the old track along the ditch which runs a bit lower down near the cliffs.

How the use of common land was controlled is not recorded, but it was no doubt consistent with the island's well established communal system of labour. The Blasket population formed a close-knit, classless society; cooperative work was common. Communal sheep farming, for example, survived the final evacuation of the island in 1953-4. Originally the Board ran barbed-wire fences along the

Map 10
Field Boundaries 1895

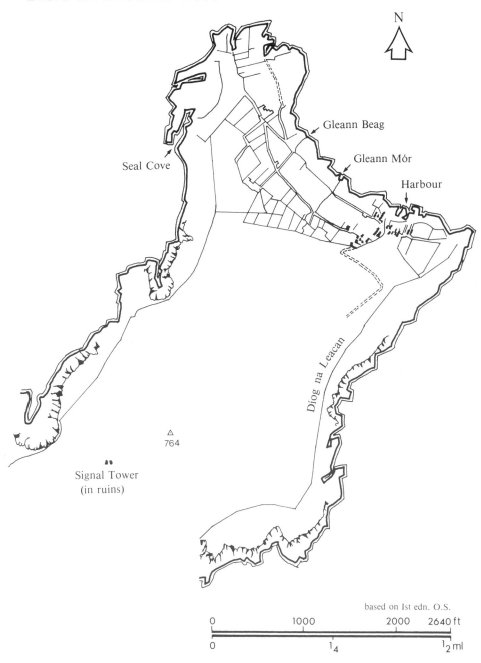

N

Seal Cove

Gleann Beag

Gleann Mór

Harbour

Díog na Leacan

△
764

Signal Tower
(in ruins)

based on Ist edn. O.S.

0   1000   2000   2640 ft

0   ¹₄   ¹₂ ml

boundary ditches, but when these fell into disuse flocks grazed in common. An individual owner's animals were identified by an interesting code of snipped ear-markings. Similar systems are found in the English Lake District and in Scandinavia. Notches and cuts of different shapes are made with a knife or the shears in one or both ears. The accompanying illustration shows some of the ear-markings used by families with flocks of sheep on the Great Blasket in the last years of the island's occupation. Shearing was, until only a few years ago, a communal activity. A party of islandmen returned to the island for two or three weeks each summer. The share-out of unmarked lambs, the system of fattening on the island of Beiginis and the supply of animals to butchers were organised on a well-understood yet informal system.

Sheep Ear Markings

(patterns used by Gt Blasket Families to indicate ownership)

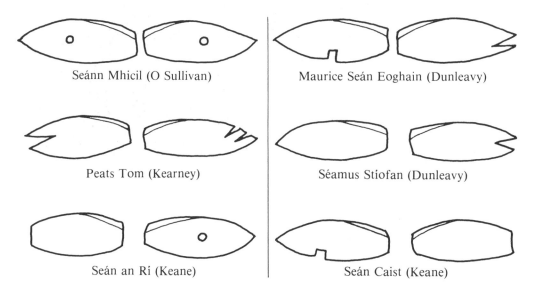

Seánn Mhicil (O Sullivan)

Maurice Seán Eoghain (Dunleavy)

Peats Tom (Kearney)

Séamus Stíofan (Dunleavy)

Seán an Rí (Keane)

Seán Caist (Keane)

*Peig "Buffer" Keane (left) and her mother Mary "Buffer" Keane,
in the mid 1930s.*

Former islanders sit among the ruins of the village.

8

The
Wild
West

What kind of people were the islanders? They have long been regarded as a special breed — wild, hardy and strange, even by nearby mainland families with whom most of them were closely related either by blood or marriage. Distinctive features by which you can recognise an islandman are still quoted by mainlanders. They are said to have uncommonly strong neck sinews from rowing with the head locked over the shoulder. They tend to walk in single file, a habit acquired on narrow island paths. As to temperament and way of life, the Blasket's own writers have provided rich documentation. Through Tomas Ó Criomhthain's recollections of oral tradition we can reach back to the middle of the last century. But to learn how the island people appeared to the outside world we have to look at other sources.

Ironically it is to the poverty of Ireland that we are indebted for the mass of travel literature dating from the nineteenth century. A flood of foreign visitors — English, Continental and American — travelled in Ireland from about 1830, attracted as much by the wretchedness and destitution of the country as by its scenery. The title of a book published in 1837 by Jonathan Binns, *The Miseries and Beauties of Ireland,* aptly summarises this paradox. A mighty population explosion and repeated famines during the late eighteenth century and the first half of the nineteenth century brought Ireland dramatically into the news. People came, both on official enquiries and at private initiative, to see for themselves the state of Ireland's poor. Some of them published accounts of their travels which provide revealing insights into social conditions. Many made a point of visiting Cork, Kerry and other distressed areas of the south and west, but the majority of these kept to the main routes, from Dublin or Cork through Waterford, Macroom, Killarney, Killorglin, Tralee, Listowel and Limerick. Occasionally they turned off for a special visit to a notoriously wretched place such as Skibbereen or Derrynane to judge for themselves the standards of the Liberator's estate management. Only a handful deviated from the Killarney-Tralee highway to push along the thirty twisting miles to Dingle town, and from there to visit villages to the west. They were rare souls indeed who made the further venture by boat into the Blasket Islands. Thus, though we have abundant descriptions of the state of the poor in many parts of Kerry, direct observations of the townlands west of Dingle and especially of the islands, are few and precious.

For centuries Ireland had been considered by the English to be barely civilised, with the possible exception of the small, fashionable elite in Dublin. To the residents of the Irish capital and the eastern seaboard, Tralee, for all its elegant Georgian streets and county gentry, was within the boundary of the known world. Dingle was an outlandish name, synonymous with the farthest end of the earth, total obscurity or Hell itself. ("He is gone to Dingle-y-Cushy.", "I wish you were in Dingly-Cushy!") In Tralee in the mid-nineteenth century, Dingle's public officials, particularly its Poor Law Guardians, were held in contempt for their slackness, corruption, nepotism and scandalous disorder. In Cork, Dingle's butter merchants and farmers were notorious for poor quality goods and every crooked trick known to the trade. Yet even Dingle ("dirty Dingle" as one visitor described it) was often scandalised by the barbarity of the parishes further west.

On 5 November 1850, the Italian brig Caroline was wrecked off the Blasket's White Strand and most of her crew drowned. On December 14 an inquest was held at Coumenoule near Dunquin on three bodies washed up on the strand there. The Dingle coroner, accompanied by a magistrate and the sub-inspector of police from Ballyferriter, suffered "much inconvenience" from the boisterous weather, "the district being very remote and wild" and from the advanced state of decomposition of the corpses. From the security of his police guard, the coroner, Mr. Justin Supple, delivered a stinging condemnation of the "barbarous inhumanity" of the local population, who had stripped the bodies of whatever wretched remnants of clothing remained on them before throwing them "like dogs in a hole without shroud or coffin".[47] An eyewitness account from Mr. Jordan, the Protestant schoolmaster then resident on the Blasket, describes how the islanders exerted themselves to save the crew so long as the ship remained intact, but when the ship broke up the crew was neglected (presumably in the rush to salvage the cargo of wheat.) Nine survivors came ashore "naked and distracted" but "the people shut their doors against them" until Patrick Kearney and William O'Shea took in three each, and Jordan the other three. Another eyewitness tells how the man who owned the land on the cliff top at Coumenoule refused to allow a grave to be dug there and threatened to throw one of the bodies back over the cliff.[48]

It is necessary for us to make allowances (as the coroner apparently did not) for the fact that after several years of the most extreme famine, sickness and destitution, the poor people of the west had become inured to all kinds of horrors, including burials in holes and ditches, or even no burials at all, not merely for ship-wrecked sailors, but for their own kith and kin. However, it appears that the islanders took the coroner's condemnation to heart. In a report on another wreck two years later, the writer took pains to emphasise the efforts the islanders, both men and women, made to warn the ship's survivors of the dangers of the White Strand and to care for them when they landed.[49]

Letters written by Lydia Jane Fisher, a Protestant lady from County Kildare, provide a number of interesting observations of the town of Dingle.[50] She described it as "a very poor place" with poverty, dirty foodshops, rats in the churchyard and much else. Of the town's inhabitants she observed, "the people appear most primitive in their notions and habits". She described a fisherman's family, which included two deaf and dumb children, living opposite her lodgings in Green Lane as "very poor and most dismally dirty . . . an Irish pigstye would be clean compared with their hovel". Of the western villages she described Ventry as being "better built and more cleanly" than neighbouring villages, apparently referring to the Protestant colony established a few years previously by the Dingle and Ventry Mission. She did not visit the Blaskets, but of particular interest is a description of the people of Dunquin which had been given to her by a Cork woman, wife of a "waterguard" (coastguardman) at Minard Castle, who had clearly suffered cultural shock on being posted to Dunquin.

> She said that Dunquin, where they were first stationed, is the wildest place in the whole wide world. The women dress like men and the men like women indiscriminately, the men wearing petticoats till they are going to be married . . . . They have no law and respect for the law, and if they mis-behave, they are so afraid of the priest that, if a rumour reaches them that he is coming, they run away and hide for days in the mountains, living on such berries and roots as they can get, until he leaves the neighbourhood.[51]

The coastguard's family was clearly the only "respectable" one in Dunquin.

Lady Chatterton, who was one of the earliest travellers on the new north coast road from Tralee to Dingle via Fermoyle and Connor Pass, describes Dunquin in 1838 as "a sad-looking little village, forlorn and desolate, fast sinking into ruin", where "the most respectable person that we saw was a person in the uniform of a coast guard".[52] Enquiring for an inn, the travellers were invited into the coastguard's own cottage for breakfast, and were delighted to find a decent house with a tidy English-looking garden and a good breakfast of tea, broiled herrings, bacon and "some very good bread and butter. The bread was a luxury

I did not expect to find in this remote place". The coastguard, Mr. Stoat, and his family were Protestants (as were most, if not all, the coastguards at this date) and clearly enjoyed a standard of housing and diet vastly superior to that of the natives.

It was no accident that the majority of visitors to the Dingle Peninsula during this period were, like the two already quoted, Protestants. During the 1830s Dingle became one of the main centres of a Protestant missionary campaign which was the cause of much publicity and controversy throughout Ireland. This Protestant campaign was the first event after the Armada wrecks of 1588 to put the Dingle Peninsula on the map of Ireland. Dingle, Ventry, and the Western villages and the so-called "Dingle Riots" and "The War in the West" became news not only in Cork and Dublin, but also in London and New York. (The leading figures in the Protestant missionary campaign were the Rev. Charles Gayer, curate of Dingle, and his convert, Thomas Moriarty. In 1844 they publicly exploited the defection to Protestantism of Fr. Brasbie, who had briefly been the Roman Catholic curate of Kilmalkedar. He was paraded round the streets of Dingle protected by police, militia, the Royal Marines and the coastguards on two Sunday mornings, occasions which have passed into history as the "Dingle Riots". No riots actually took place, except in Protestant imagination, but the episode typifies the type of spectacular propaganda employed by the missionary leaders in Dingle — the public exhibition of converts at the particularly sensitive hour on Sunday morning when all the men and boys of the town would be lining the main streets after Mass.) It is partly to this religious controversy that the increased literary coverage of the mid-century is due, either directly from the writings of the actual protagonists, or indirectly from the records of outside observers. Naturally, those actively engaged in a local struggle are not unbiased witnesses, but from the impassioned propaganda small details can be extracted which have the ring of truth.

Mrs. A. M. Thompson's book, *A Brief Account of the Rise and Progress of the Change in Religious Opinion Now Taking Place in Dingle,* was published in London in 1846. The author was the wife of Lord Ventry's land-agent, David Peter Thompson, who moved to the Dingle area from Tralee in the 1830s. She was believed by local Catholics to have been one of the prime movers in the proselytising campaign. Mrs. Thompson's book contains much interesting material. She had a genuine interest in people and a keen eye for detail, and from her we get some vivid, if brief, observations of the country people who crowded into the first improvised Soupers' schoolroom in Ventry. They appeared as "creatures who for uncivilised aspect and poverty of garb might bear comparison with the most savage nations. The women squatted on the floor nursing their infants — older infants were supplied with a potato or perhaps a live bird to keep them quiet." Potatoes and live birds as playthings and the practice of squatting on the haunches *(ar a chorraghiob)* are fully attested in living memory. Mrs. Thompson visited the Great Blasket in 1840 or soon after. The purpose of her visit was to see and report on the new school and teacher's house which the Dingle and Ventry Mission had just built with funds she herself had raised in England for that purpose. She writes that not one of the 150 inhabitants could read or write. Other promoters of conversion describe the islanders of this period in general terms ("the wildest and most uncultivated people in our land"), but Mrs. Thompson's account of her meeting with the island women moves from generalisation into marvellously detailed observation:

> I was more affected than I have power to describe, by witnessing human nature reduced to the savage state it is among these islanders. When I got into the new schoolroom, the women and children in great numbers crowded in and squatted themselves on the floor round me, chewing sea weed incessantly, a large supply of which was in every woman's pocket and lap, and of which they pressed the long strings into their mouths with their thumbs in a most savage manner, and spat about unceremoniously at will, they touched my dress, turned me round and round to look at every separate article, laughed with admiration at my shoes and gloves, kissed and stroked my old silk gown, repeating 'Bragh! Bragh!' 'nice, nice!' though the reader may believe I did not wear anything very handsome on such an expedition.[53]

Again, the details are entirely authentic: the squatting, the constant chewing of seaweed (probably dilisc) and the touching evidence in these roughened women of that universal feminine delight in clothes and fine fabrics. The physical handling not only of the fabrics but of the lady herself demonstrates the good-humoured tolerance of the visitor and, on the part of the women, a freedom of manners arising not so much from incivility as from a natural assumption of common interest, recalling Kipling's poem *The Ladies*. A similar incident was experienced by Mrs. Fisher in the church porch at Kilmalkedar a few years earlier:

> As I took shelter there from a shower, an old woman approached me, looked very inquisitively at my face and dress, took my gown in her hand, felt it, examined it carefully, then inspected the petticoat and turned away. She could not speak a word of English. I felt very awkward while undergoing the scrutiny, for I could not speak a word of Irish.[54]

Visits to the western townlands from ladies in gowns, petticoats and shoes were obviously rare.

When Mrs. Thompson directed the island women's reluctant attention to more serious matters such as sin and redemption, she had an active audience. Whereas the Ventry congregation (better disciplined in the presence of two clergymen, members of Lord Ventry's family and other gentry) confined its participation to nodding, smiling and groaning, the Blasket women argued vigorously in defence of the hereditary religion. Their thinking was concrete: Mrs. Thompson was shocked to find that their definition of "sin" was "sheep-stealing", no doubt reflecting the most significant commodity in the island's economy at that time. The whole episode indicated the same lively openness and independence in the island character at this period which became familiar to many later visitors. Similarly, the Reverend Mr. Foley, inspector for the Irish Missionary Society and himself a native of Dingle, was startled by the active participation of the congregation at Kilmalkedar when he preached there in 1844. "They appear to be a most interesting flock . . . I was a little disconcerted during the sermon . . . at hearing most of the people respond aloud in the affirmative to some of my observations."

In John Windele's description of Mrs. Thomas Keane of Inis Tuaisceart (Margaret Dunlea or Dunleavy), we have a first-hand impression of an individual island woman of this period: "bare and elastic of foot". As we know from the parish records, however, she was the mother of at least eight children at the time of his visit in 1838, and most of them had been born and reared in an ancient clochán, a primitive semi-subterranean cell barely eleven feet in diameter. The family had lived, alone for the most part, on this isolated island for twelve years or more. Windele says nothing about Mrs. Keane's appearance beyond conveying an impression of vigour and agility. Clearly he regarded her situation as pitiable. Particularly interesting is the survival in this poor woman, living in sub-human conditions, of the old Gaelic tradition of hospitality, of her personal dignity and generosity towards strangers with whatever resources (rabbits and sea birds) she had.[55]

The Blasket way of life during the late nineteenth century and the first three decades of the present century has been fully documented by island writers including Tomás Ó Criomhthain, Maurice O'Sullivan and Peig Sayers as well as several later writers such as Robin Flower. Most of these books are in print once again, and we strongly urge the reader to turn to these for the true, salty flavour of the island community. We need only quote from a few outside observations from this period which are not so easily accessible.

Sam Hussey (1821-1910) was the last of a string of Husseys to act as agent for the absentee Earl of Cork and Orrery who owned the Blaskets. Sam succeeded his elder brother Edward (d.1864) in this post and pursued a hard line during the Land War of the last three

Ancient clochán on Inis Tuaisceart.

Above: Interior of the "Buffer" Keane house circa 1934. This was one of the new houses put up by the County Council at the top of the village.

Right: Nellie Daly Carney and her daughter Maureen. Nellie was a mainlander from Dunquin who married Seán-Tom Kearney in 1914, after he had done two five-year stints in America. They had ten living children before Nellie died circa 1936.

decades of the nineteenth century. He was responsible for some of the confrontations between islanders and bailiffs recorded by Tomás Ó Criomhthain. He is said to have evicted half the island tenants in 1880 for the non-payment of rent, and in 1890 he impounded the island's only two fishing-boats for the same reason. This action, which deprived the islanders of their only source of income, was followed by an outbreak of fever and the failure of the potato crop on the island.[56] It appears from the estate papers handed over to the Congested Districts Board in 1907 that no rent had been collected for at least eleven and a half years, since 1895, and that the rent had been only intermittently paid before that. A writer in 1880 (no doubt primed by Mr. Hussey himself), described all twenty-five Blasket families as "squatters" who exceeded all others in poverty, misery and lawlessness.[57]

In his autobiography, *Reminiscences of an Irish Landagent*, Sam Hussey reveals his view of the Blasket people as social parasites, and deceitful and grasping peasants. He alleged that the island people resisted collection not only of rent, but also of poor rates and county cess. Yet despite all his years as landlord's agent, Mr. Hussey does not quote a single personal contact with any of the island people. Such anecdotes as he tells of them are jokes of the comic Irish peasant type, in which the characters speak in a sort of music-hall Anglo-Irish. The expression "illegant" appears with suspicious frequency. To illustrate their shameless duplicity Hussey tells how the islanders applied for relief from two charities simultaneously in 1880, the Duchess of Marlborough's and the Dublin Mansion House Fund. Asked how the islanders were getting on, a Blasket man, according to Mr. Hussey, replied: "Illegant, glory be to the Saints! We're eating the Duchess and feeding the pigs on the Mansion House."[58]

In J. M. Synge, who stayed on the Great Blasket Island for several weeks during August and September 1905, the islanders had a more sympathetic observer. Synge was struck by the contrasting elements in the island character — gaiety and melancholy, kindliness and severity, roughness and delicacy, boldness and reserve. He noted the curious seriousness with which they danced, the open sociable atmosphere of the king's kitchen where a neighbour dropped in to warm some milk for her baby when her own fire was out, where the men gathered for communal hair-cutting and shaving on a Saturday night, where thirty or more people would crowd in for talk or music of an evening. Food, furniture, games, dances, the almost universal use of tobacco, including the smoking of cigarettes by a group of older girls are noted, as well as attitudes and personalities, in a series of impressions recorded in rough notebooks during his stay. His observations formed the basis for part of his article on West Kerry published a few years later. His general impression of the islanders was of "kindly, beaming faces . . . the most hearty,

good-natured and merry people I have met anywhere".[59] His opinion
was echoed by Peig Sayers, who, although she eventually became one
of the island's most celebrated writers, came in as a stranger at the age
of seventeen or eighteen:

> There is no question but there was a pleasant company on the
> island in those days . . . . That's the way they were then, and that's
> the way they are now, though there are many people who imagine
> that it is wild they are in the island. Quiet, honest, warm-hearted,
> hospitable folk they are, and the stranger will find friendship and
> kindliness — if not, when the fault's in himself.[60]

A small instance of faith in the friendliness and honesty of the
Blasket people appears in an unconfirmed story quoted in the *Kerry
Evening Post* in 1848, the year in which a temporary work house was
opened in Dingle. By the autumn it was grossly overcrowded, and there
were complaints from indignant rate-payers that many families
supported by the rates were receiving money from relatives in America.
Since the possession of even a few pence automatically disqualified
applicants from relief, such people would go to great lengths to conceal
the receipt of letters from the United States (with the active
participation, it was claimed, of the Dingle post-master). One woman
who had received American money had her relief stopped. When she
applied to have it restored she swore upon oath "that she had not a
penny at this side of the water" — truthfully, since "she had taken care
to lodge the money with a friend in the Blasquet Island a few days
before".[61]

The Blasket Islands from the mountain road from Dunquin to Ventry Chapel.

Peig Sayers in 1947.

9

The Flowering of Literary Talent

The Great Blasket Island is today known throughout the world because it was the home of three Irish writers — Tomás Ó Criomhthain, Peig Sayers, and Maurice O'Sullivan. None of them had more than a basic village school education, yet their writings have delighted men and women from all walks of life. It is one of the curiosities of their fame that although in Ireland they are rightly admired as writers in Irish, they are known chiefly through the English translations of their works. The English scholars, notably Robin Flower, Kenneth Jackson, and George Thomson, who encouraged their work, however, would never have known these islanders except for West Kerry's thoroughly deserved reputation for pure Irish speech and traditional Irish lore. They would never have suggested that they write autobiographies if they had not been so impressed through conversation and friendship with the islanders' wonderful natural capacity for telling a good story.

There is in the writings of all three a genuine novelty, a new flowering of literary talent and it is this that has made them so famous. They put the traditional art of story-telling to new use. No longer is it concerned strictly with legends of the ancient past, of fantasies about fairies (though Peig, for one, refers to these, and indeed recorded an enormous number of such tales). Instead their stories deal with the realities of their own life and times, with real dangers of cliff and sea, with flesh-and-blood heroes of seal-hunting and storms, with salty comments on neighbours still living or recently dead. All are told with wit and vigour, and are based on sharp, precise observation. One of the most powerful fascinations of their books is the picture they give of a way of life which though "modern" in a historical sense is nevertheless completely different from that of nearly every reader. A culture in which marriages are arranged by match-makers; a community in which there are no class divisions; a society which knows a few simple tools, but has no machines. Yet even this statement needs qualification. As an old woman in 1937, Peig Sayers had no hesitation in hitching a lift in a motor car on her first trip to Ballyferriter since her marriage there forty-two years before.[62]

The three island writers, Tomás Ó Criomhthain, Peig Sayers and

*Gobnait ní Chinnéide (left) and Meini, the storyteller, who was married
to Seán Owen Dunleavy (Seán Fada in most of the island narratives).
Meini was also a midwife of no small reputation and most of the islanders
say they wouldn't be in the world but for her.*

Maurice O'Sullivan, form an interesting trio. Their three most famous books, *The Islandman, Peig* and *Twenty Years A-Growing,* were all published (in Irish) in the short space of six years, between 1929 and 1935, yet there is a gap of almost twenty years between the dates of birth of the first two writers (1856 for Tomás and 1873 for Peig), and just over twenty years between Peig and Maurice, who was born in 1904. All three share certain attractive qualities — a conversational directness, vivid narrative and sharp observation (of self and others) — yet each is distinctive. *The Islandman* is obviously an old man's book, while *Twenty Years A-Growing* is clearly the work of a young man. Peig manages to give an elderly woman's view over a long span of life, and yet she recaptures as completely as Maurice O'Sullivan the zest of childhood and youth; indeed she never lost it.

The two men were born and bred on Great Blasket. Tomás Ó Criomhthain lived there all his seventy-one years, and that gives his book a fascinating narrowness of view. He cannot help but reveal "the things that have meant most to me", as he says in the last chapter of his book, for he has no standards of contrast or comparison with other styles of life, either on the mainland (as Peig had, for she did not go to the Blasket until two days after her wedding), or in the city (as Maurice had, young as he was when he wrote his book). The concluding chapters of *Twenty Years A-Growing* describe Maurice's training as a Civic Guard in Dublin, but one feels that the experience of life in the city only heightened his sense of the unique way of life he had left behind. Maurice's book is the most ecstatic in its descriptions of the natural beauty of the Blaskets, though Peig comes a close second. Tomás Ó Criomhthain, by contrast, is much more concerned with the dangers of the sea and the hardships of life on the island. His anxieties as a husband and father making a livelihood in this inhospitable place dominate his outlook. All three excitedly and unashamedly tell about the great improvement in their standard of living brought by the Great War of 1914-18 — the bountiful harvest of all sorts of goods brought in on the tides from torpedoed merchantmen.

All three writers offer reflective comments on their experiences: sometimes it is no more than an apposite instance of proverbial wisdom, as when Peig is grieving over the loss of a fourth child and remarks "It has been said that there is no joy in life without its own sorrow to accompany it". But at other times it is an entirely original observation. There was that touching moment, for example, when Maurice O'Sullivan, as a small boy at school and in trouble with his foster-mother, asked himself "When would the day come when I would be a man, free from the control of matrons, no school to sicken me and the mistress beating me no more?" There is a knock at the door, and a poor, wet vagabond woman comes in with two bedraggled children, soon to be followed by two burly constables who arrest her and lead her away. Maurice comments, "All this time I was watching them and I began thinking again, as I listened to her going away from the house shouting and crying, that it was a queer world — a full-grown woman like her to be under control the same as myself."

There is no end to the comparisons and contrasts that one might make between the work of these three highly individual writers, but we would like to conclude this chapter by examining one quality they all share and two topics they all treat, which, in our view, have rightly established the popularity of their books, and will ensure that they continue to be read.

First, they are all excellent story-tellers. They have an assured touch. Their stories are interesting in themselves, dealing with clashes of personality, dilemmas of everyday life, sudden reversals of fortune. They move at a good pace, and are spiced with sharp, often ironic observation. Examples include Peig's account of the puppy stealing and breaking her clay pipe when she was desperate for a smoke, and then she herself breaking another as it slipped from her almost tooth-less jaws; or Tomás's tobacco tale about Pats Hamish, who, the worse for drink, courteously addresses a wooden model of a woman in Atkins's shop in Dingle. Tomás introduces him as "the sort of man that couldn't keep a glass of whisky or a pint of porter long between his hands without pouring them down him, and he never enjoyed the taste of anything he paid for with his own money, but liked it well when another man jogged him in the back to have one with him." Or Maurice's vivid account of an idyllic day's hunt for rabbits and puffins at the far end of the island, or his account of the Ventry Races with its galaxy of characters — gamblers, singers, tricksters, musicians — and the two boys each drinking two pints out of bravado, feeling dizzy, throwing up and then feeling "as well as ever — but I tell you I cursed the man who first thought of porter." It is a constant delight to the reader to find the traditional Irish gift for telling stories used to make vivid incidents of everyday life.

All three writers dwell on the recreations of island people, their diversions from the hardships of life. There are, of course, many stories of drinking and revelry. All, for example, mention days of multiple marriages at Ballyferriter, but it is what went on in the bars and the street, not in the church, that is described. All recall with delight the singing they have heard; Peig lovingly recording the words of the songs. Young Maurice tells how much he enjoyed his grandad's singing when he first rejoined his family on the island; it prompted his first words of Irish "mo gradgo deo bu" ("My love forever!"). And Tomás wistfully tells of the sweet singing of the girl from the Inis he didn't marry, sitting with her mother in a bar in Dingle.

Robin Flower and Tomás Ó Criomhthain.

Maurice O'Sullivan in Civic Guard uniform with
George Thomson, his translator.

One topic that fascinates many readers is the custom of match-making — the ritual praises of the groom by the match-maker, the prolonging of the negotiations with song and drink, the speed with which the marriage follows the concluding of the match, the willing acceptance of the match by the couple involved, even if, like Peig, they may not have exchanged a word together before the match was made; the fact that a young lad like Maurice is allowed to listen in on the gossip of the "old hags" involved in the match-making; the way a young man of feeling, like Tomás, allowed his own preference to be over-ruled by his sister; the strength and stability of the marriages contracted in this way. Much, of course, is omitted. Despite the deep respect and affection Peig obviously had for her husband, he is a shadowy figure compared with many other characters in her book. Peig gives hardly more than a phrase or two of his speech and no hint of the nuances of his character. We are shocked, in both Peig's and Tomás's books, to find the deaths of husband and wife and several children all dealt with in a few brief sentences, when a whole chapter can be devoted to an account of an outing to Ventry or Dingle. But perhaps these very reticences indicate most powerfully of all the gulf between their view of life and ours.

Tomás states at the end of his book: "I have written minutely of much that we did, for it was my wish that somewhere there should be a memorial of it all, and I have done my best to set down the character of the people about me so that some record of us might live after us, for the like of us will never be again." Similarly Peig remarks at the end of her autobiography "Old as I am, there's a great deal more in my head that I can't write down here. I did my best to give an accurate account of the people I knew, so that we'd be remembered when we had moved on into eternity. People will yet walk above our heads; it could even happen that they'd walk into the graveyard where I'll be lying but people like us will never again be there." Between them, these three island writers have given us a remarkable picture of a distinctive and now vanished way of life.

Island sheep with Tearacht looming in the distance.

10

The Outer Islands

The Great Blasket is well named. It is a magnificent island in its own right. Yet anyone who gazes out to the Great Blasket from the mainland must also be struck by the appropriateness of the existence of five satellite outer islands. The Great Blasket deserves the homage of these lesser Blasket islands. The title "Great" is doubly fitting.

Visually, the smaller islands provide a dramatic setting for the Great Blasket. Each one has its own special features, from the rocky and barren pyramid of remote Tearacht (a quite unearthly Gothic shape) to the extraordinarily flat and lush Beiginis lying just a few hundred yards from the White Strand of the main island. Each island has acquired its own collection of tales — half history, half legend — passed on by word of mouth over several generations. Very little documentary evidence relating to their history has come to light, and no thorough archaeological investigation has as yet been undertaken on any of them (or, for that matter, on the Great Blasket Island). Nevertheless, we do know with absolute certainty that all five of them — Inishvickillaune, Inis na Bró, Tearacht, Tuaisceart, and Beiginis — despite being even more inhospitable than the parent island, had inhabitants intermittently throughout the nineteenth century and most, if not all, have been places of human habitation in the more remote past.

The evidence for nineteenth century settlements is threefold — oral tradition, the ten-yearly and other censuses from 1841 onwards, and the Baptismal Registers of the Parish of Ballyferriter, of which all the islands are a part. Our excitement was high when, in August 1972, we started to work our way through the "Liber Baptizatum Parochiarum:— Kilmelckidar, Morhin, Kilqane, Dunurlin et Dunquin 1808-1828", the oldest surviving baptismal register for the parish, looking for Blasket Island entries and found that the first was not for a child from "Insula Magna" (the Great Island), but for Catherine Gueehin, daughter of Joannis Gueehin and Maria Duana of "Insulae tli Kyliani" (Inishvickillaune). The date of the entry was 5 April 1808. Catherine Gueehin was the first of thirteen children born on that remote island between 1808 and 1895 and brought the long journey by sea and land to Ballyferriter to be baptised.

Four of the Blasket Island group from 15,000 feet. From left to right: Inishvickillaune, Inis na Br

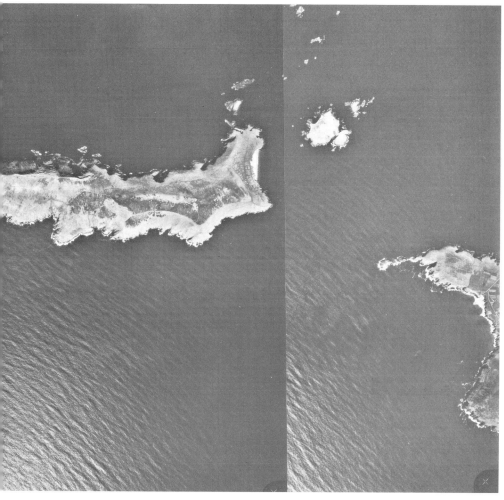

at Blasket, Beiginis and bottom right the mainland of Kerry — Dunmore Head and Slea Head.

117

INISHVICKILLAUNE

Though the furthest west of all (except for the rock Tearacht), Inishvickilluane is the island most readily seen from the mainland east of Dingle. Once you have come over the Connor Pass from the north side of the peninsula, and turned into the long straight that leads to Dingle itself, the southern half of Inishvickillaune peers at you (on a clear day) round the mass of Slea Head, shimmering across the ocean from a distance of twenty miles.

After the Great Blasket, it is the island that has been visited most often and the one that has exercised the most powerful fascination on those who have been there. It has an attractive shape — a lovely smooth grassy headland to the northwest overlooking fine rocky cliffs, and in the middle jagged heights from which superb views can be gained in all directions. The Great Blasket and the mainland lie to the east, the Skelligs and the Ring of Kerry to the south, Inis na Bró to the north, and the limitless Atlantic to the west. A charming tumble of fields on the southeast of Inishvickillaune balances the unfenced headland of the other side of the island. In the centre of the island are the monastic ruins listed by the antiquaries — a roofless oratory chapel and numerous grave sites — all much plundered for the making of field walls. There is no clear indication now of how many buildings there were originally, nor how they were disposed. In all, the island is barely a mile in length and a half a mile broad.

One solitary early document mentioning this island has so far come to light. It is found in the Register of the Hospital of St. John the Baptist in Dublin. It dates from the early thirteenth century and is a deed of gift from Adam Dundno of a mark of silver owed to him by Ricardus de Marisc "annuatim de Insula de Hynchemacyvelan" ("as annual rent for the island of Inishvickillaune). But that is all. We do not know to what use, if any, the island was put at that time. Charles Smith in *The Ancient and Present State of the County of Kerry*, published in 1756, states emphatically that "the island being low and too bleak to afford shelter there have been none here for many years past".[63] However, he does mention "the ruins of an ancient chapel, in which an old chalice and a baptismal font of stone still remain and likewise a cell similar to the Galerus".[64]

The next written comment we have is a very brief one. In 1838 John Windele, who visited Tuaisceart with Father Casey (the beloved parish priest of Ballyferriter), merely says that Inishvickillaune "is a great place for breeding eagles".[65] In 1856 the island was visited by George du Noyer who made a water colour sketch of a cross-inscribed ogham stone there, and wrote: "The island is systematically farmed, and always stocked with sheep; a family of six or eight

Dry-stone ruins on Inishvickillaune.

Aerial view of Inishvickillaune in 1977 showing Mr. Haughey's house being built (bottom left) as well as the ruined oratory (square-looking building to right of photo).

inhabited it at the time of my visit . . . these people assert that during one stormy season their fire went out, and, not having the means of relighting it, they were reduced almost to starvation; they, however, supported life for a period of two months by the use of sheep's milk alone."[66] The keeping of sheep on the island in the mid-nineteenth century is confirmed in a story told by Tomás Ó Criomhthain's father about John Hussey, the land agent, who took "two boats' crews of us to Inishvickillaune to shear sheep".[67] They spent three days on the job, which suggests a goodly flock of sheep. Robin Flower, in *The Western Island*, comments that the soil of Inishvickillaune, though too rich for potatoes, is good for cabbages and onions, and that even tobacco has been grown there.[68]

Everyone who has written about the Inis, as the island is commonly called by Great Blasket people, has included stories about the appearance of spirits of the dead and of fairies. The fairies that Maurice O'Sullivan heard, however, turned out to be seals and petrels! There is a delightful story, told by Robin Flower, and repeated by others, of the man on the Inis who, as he was sitting in his house, soothing his loneliness with a fiddle "heard another music without, going over the roof in the air. It passed away to the cliffs and returned again, and so backwards and forwards again and again, a wandering air wailing in repeated phrases, till at last it had become familiar in his mind, and he took up with the fallen bow, and drawing it across the strings followed note by note the lamenting voices as they passed above him."[69] That tune is now known as *port na bpúcaí* ("the fairy music"), and is one of the most popular tunes today in the Dingle Peninsula.

Throughout the nineteenth century, and into the early twentieth century, the Inis intermittently supported one or more families. Thirteen children, belonging to the Guiheen, Sheehy, Shea, and Daly families, were born there between 1808 and 1882. The Daly family remained on the island until 1903 or 1904, when, most of the children having gone to the United States, they moved to the Great Blasket. In 1904 J. M. Synge visited the Great Blasket Island and reported that Maurice Daly, the father of Paddy Daly who had set up as a carpenter and canoe-builder on the Great Blasket, "an old man of eighty years is going to spend the winter alone on Inishvickillaune. . . ."[70] Despite moving to the Great Blasket Island, and later to Dunquin, the Dalys have continued to keep sheep on the Inis, making trips by currach to shear them and bring back their fleece to the mainland. While on the island they use the cosy stone house that nestles below the well, near the centre of the island, which has almost certainly been there since the early nineteenth century.

During the First World War young men from the Great Blasket occasionally took refuge on the Inis to avoid military service. Early in the Second World War, on 28 November 1940, a German bomber came down in the sea not far from the pebble beach on the east side of the Inis.[71] The five crew members all got safely to the island in two rubber dinghies and spent three nights there. They then paddled their dinghies across Black Sound to Ceann Dubh at the western end of the Great Blasket, and two of them climbed Hawk's Cliff, using knotted ropes to make the ascent. The Germans came to the village and "spoke" to the islanders in sign language and gave them cigarettes. The pilot then accompanied some of the islanders to the mainland, where they were met by Irish soldiers. Eventually an Irish naval vessel came to the Great Blasket and removed the other four men. They all spent the rest of the war in internment.

In the past few years a new house has been built on the Inis, with materials brought in by boat and helicopter. It is the Atlantic home of the erstwhile Taoiseach, Charles Haughey.

INIS NA BRÓ

Inis na Bró, near neighbour to Inishvickillaune, also has a splendid shape. It is a great grassy saddle, rising to huge humps in the southeast and northwest. If you pass it by sea en route from the Great Blasket to Inishvickillaune you obtain a view of the massive pinnacles of rock at its northern tip with daylight showing through jagged holes at sea level. Very little is known of the history of human habitation of the island. No baptisms were recorded for it in the nineteenth century, although the 1851 census records one family (two males, two females) living there "in one house" — perhaps, as on Inis Tuaisceart, a beehive hut. Their stay must have been short-lived. The families on Inishvickillaune, however, used the island for grazing half-grown lambs and made frequent expeditions there to hunt rabbits and seabirds. The island is very difficult of access: there is no harbour or landing beach.

TEARACHT

Tearacht, the next island in the arc around the Great Blasket from west to north, is little more than a great rock some 600 feet high. It is almost entirely devoid of vegetation, though a small terrace may once have been an area of cultivation, like the "monastery garden" on Skellig Michael, an island Tearacht in many ways resembles though on a much smaller scale. There are oral traditions of a monastic settlement on the Tearacht, but no archaeological investigation has yet been made to put that tradition to the test. Also like Skellig Michael it has a lighthouse, which was first built in 1870. The island is mentioned in the Griffith Valuation Tenure Book of 1850, and there is a record of it having been bought by the Port of Dublin Corporation from the Earl of Cork on

Rocks off Inishvickillaune.

Ruins on Inis Tuaisceart.

15 September 1864, for the sum of £200.[72] Seventy-five pounds of that sum went to Miss Clara Hussey "for her interest in the place". Miss Hussey was the sister of the land agent who took island men to the Inis for sheep shearing. For the modern visitor on the mainland, the Tearacht appears as an astonishing distant rock, more fantasy than reality, far out in the Atlantic, a final punctuation mark to Europe. Beyond it westwards is the vastness of the ocean — "next parish America".

TUAISCEART

While Tearacht is the most distant of the outer Blasket islands, Tuaisceart is the most isolated, lying as it does three miles to the north of the east-west line of the other islands. It is also an island with remarkable physical features, in particular an enormous rock spire rising from its northern cliffs which you cannot see from the mainland until you have passed north of Clogher Head. From Coumenoule or the Great Blasket Island, Tuaisceart, strikingly resembles a reclining figure with feet to the west, head to the east, and hands folded across its stomach in the middle.

Like Inishvickillaune, Tuaisceart has substantial remains of stone buildings, presumed to be of monastic origin, which were mentioned by Charles Smith as early as 1756, and noted in some detail by both John Windele and George du Noyer, who visited the island in 1838 and 1856 respectively. The largest of these ruined buildings has been given the title of "the oratory". However, so far no references to any Blasket monastic settlements have yet been found in manuscripts that date back to the early centuries of the Christian era (as they have for Skellig Michael), so we can only guess about their original date of construction, and their links with one another. Like Inishvickillaune this island also has considerable remains of field walls scattered in the area of the ruins of the ancient buildings. The beehive hut known as St. Brendan's Cell or Clochán which lies almost in the centre of this island, was inhabited early in the nineteenth century. There are nine entries for the island in the baptismal registers of Ballyferriter, dating from 1815 to 1838 and relating to five different families. Windele in his account of his visit there in 1838 tells of the hospitable reception given him and Father Casey by Mrs. Keane (her husband was away at the time on the mainland), but unfortunately does not give any description of the interior of the beehive hut she lived in or of its furnishings.[73] The space is just over eleven feet in diameter, and Tomás Ó Criomhthain is not alone in wondering how a family (and probably animals too) managed to live in it.

It seems clear that human occupation of the island during this period was intermittent, families coming from and returning to the

Great Blasket. The 1841 census shows no one living on the island at that time, but another family did settle on the island in the late 1840s or early 1850s. This occupation ended in tragedy. The gruesome details are provided by du Noyer. He says that in about 1850:

> this island was used as a sheep farm, and a married couple were left there in charge, who lived in St. Brendan's Cloghaun. An unusual spell of stormy weather having occurred, the constant visits of the Dunquin boatmen were interrupted, and no communication with the people of the island could be attempted for about six weeks. When the place was at length visited, a fearful spectacle presented itself: the woman was alone, nearly dead from hunger, and a maniac; around her in the dark lay clots of blood and lumps of putrid flesh, the remains of her husband. After a time, when she partially recovered her senses, the sad story was elicited, that during the bad weather her husband sickened and died, and being a very large and robust man, she had not the strength to remove the body from the hut, up the steep flight of steps; for many weary days and nights she sat by the corpse, till its presence became intolerable; there was no other shelter but this hut on the island, and in despair she dismembered the decaying mass, and buried the pieces singly without. Since then the place has been deserted, and even sheep are rarely left to pasture there.[74]

It is hardly surprising that subsequent occupation of the island was sporadic and brief.

The chapel on the island, according to Father Casey in a letter he wrote to John Windele in 1839 was formerly "almost as perfect and uninjured as the one at Galerus." But "the fellow at present living there" had apparently taken stone from it "to fence his tillage garden".[75]

BEIGINIS

The final member of the outer islands, Beiginis, is utterly different from the others in both character and appearance. It is just a flat slice of land some thirty-six acres in extent whose "cliffs" never rise more than thirty feet above sea level. It is very lush in grass, but does not contain a single well. And whereas all the other islands have an obvious independence of their own, Beiginis is very much under the lee of the Great Blasket and protected by it from the westerly gales that sweep across the others. Like the other islands it is referred to by Charles Smith in his *History of Kerry* (1756). He described it as "a very fertile spot . . . that will fatten 30 bullocks every summer, the grass is mostly clover and cinquefoil, and is constantly enriched by the spray of the sea, which always leaves a considerable quantity of salt behind it."[76] In more recent times it has been used for fattening sheep from the

Beiginis, the smallest of the Blasket group, as seen from the ruined village.

Inis na Bró from Inishvickillaune.

Great Blasket to ready them for sheep markets on the mainland. Peig Sayers, at the beginning of *An Old Woman's Reflections,* tells how boats used to go there from the Great Blasket to cut seaweed, and Tomás Ó Criomhthain speaks of men from Iveragh who one year fished for lobsters making the island of Beiginis their base, and living in a "shanty" there.[77] This would be in the 1870s.

The lack of drinking water on this otherwise suitable and accessible island (there is a convenient, sheltered inlet on the south side), has militated strongly against its use as a place for human habitation. Some time early in the nineteenth century the landlord, Peig Sayers tells us, decided to build "milk houses" in the Dunquin area and built one of them on Beiginis. The ruins of this handsome building (it was some sixty feet long) can still be seen. The baptismal records show that a daughter was born to John Kavan and Bridget Ferriter on Beiginis in 1824, but when their second child was baptized in 1827 they were living on the Great Blasket. In May 1830 a child born to Thomas Mannin and Catherine Long of Beiginis was baptised; but these are the only entries in the baptismal registers. According to Peig, Richard O'Carroll and Kate Daly looked after cows and ran the dairy for the landlord at a somewhat later date. Because there was no well, Richard used to row over barrels of water from the Great Blasket, but he was drowned one day in rough weather after which his widow left the island. It does not seem that the dairy continued after that time. Tomás Ó Criomhthain, however, reports that the Great Blasket people used Beiginis for fattening cattle, and there are tales of cows and bulls swimming from Beiginis back to the Great Blasket, much to the astonishment of their owners.

From all the outer islands the eye is drawn back to the Great Blasket, a larger, more splendid and complex reclining figure than any of them. It is no wonder that the islanders who in past years ventured even farther away from the main stream of human life to these outer islands should in the end have returned to the parent island.

Island woman Máire , married to Thomas Kearney, was one of the most famous grandmothers on the island and was an associate of Peig's.

11
A
National
Park?

The earliest mention of the Great Blasket Island so far discovered dates from the thirteenth century, when it was owned by the Earl of Desmond. It is recorded that he leased it to the Ferriter family for an annual rent of two hawks. In the sixteenth century, at the end of the Desmond rebellion, his forfeited lands were allotted to the supporters of the Crown, passing eventually, in this instance, to Sir Richard Boyle, later Earl of Cork. The Great Blasket Island remained part of that family's Irish and Orrery estate until the beginning of the twentieth century. In 1907 the then Earl of Cork sold the Island to the Congested Districts Board, the British Government's agency for matters of this sort in Ireland. The deed of sale, which is preserved in Dublin, gives details of the transaction. It shows that the earl made over completely all his interests in the island.

To go back over the three hundred years of the tenure of the successive Earls of Cork, it seems very unlikely that any of those who had this legal title to the island ever visited it personally. The one reference that has come down to us is that in 1736 the then Earl, during a visit to his extensive estates in Ireland, reported seeing from the mainland 'some tillage and a few cabins, whence, during the time I was looking at the island, some poor wretches entered into a boat with rabbits for sale.' He would hardly have expected much rent from such poor people.

However, in the 170 years that followed this episode a substantial village came into being on the island, with many new houses being built and older houses improved. The earlier picture of a simple, desolate island, hardly worthy of a note in the cataloguing of a rich man's estates, had changed rapidly. Not only had the population increased to over 150, but the arable land to the north of the village had been enclosed and divided into sixty-six fields. Each field was allocated quite precisely to one or other of the family houses, whose owners are named in the deed of transfer of the island from the Earl of Cork to the CDB, with the rents due from each varying from £2 to £6 per annum.

The Earl was paid £600 by the British Government for the island in

The general exhibition area of the Blasket Centre, which is called 'An Slí'.
This long hallway overlooks the village on the Great Blasket Island.

that year, 1907. Considering that all his tenants were between six and twelve years in arrears with their rents he may well have been satisfied with the deal. Among other things, the deed of sale designates the nine-tenths of the island's area that lies to the west of the village and fields as 'common pasturage', with each householder having a 1/25th share in its use.

What is not found in this document is any reference to the responsibility for the maintenance of the island – its roads, wells and water drainage ditches – or of the harbour, though we know that from time to time public money was provided for improvements of one sort or another after 1906; for example, for the erection of the two storey 'government houses' at the top of the village, in the period 1910 to 1917.

It could well be that at the time the transfer of the island to the CDB in 1907 there was felt to be no need for any specification of the responsibility for public services, in view of the fact that the island villagers themselves had already for many decades established their own unwritten, informal, but very effective system of mutual co-operation in these matters.

With the establishment of the Irish Free State in 1922, the functions of the CDB were passed to the Irish Land Commission, who gave all the island families rights of freehold. This ushered in a new and more complex period of ownership. Now each of the twenty-five freeholders owned not only his family house, but also the two or three fields that went with it, and his share in the common pasturage to the west of the village. At the time this made no significant difference to the pattern of life on the island. Work together on land and sea continued in exactly the same way as it had done before.

The following two decades – roughly the twenties and thirties of the last century – can be regarded in two quite different lights. Either, as the golden period of the Island's history, with the flowering of literary talent as manifested in the works of Tomas Ó Criomhtháin and Peig Sayers and Muiris Ó Suilleabhain, and the international fame that came to the island with the translation of the works of these authors into English, or, on the other hand, as the sunset of its history, with the steady tide of emigration of young people to the USA, and the failure of any new families to be established on the island after 1921.

The decline of the village after World War II was extremely rapid. The number of children in the school dropped to a handful, houses were abandoned as families moved to the mainland, taking their furniture and often the roofs of their house with them. This culminated in 1953 with the complete evacuation of the twenty-three remaining inhabitants. All these island families were rehoused by the government on the mainland, four of them in Dunquin. However, the government did not, in

Islanders step ashore at Dingle after the evacuation

exchange, take over these families' freehold rights on the island. I think we can assume they were thought to be worthless.

After 1953 the islandmen who had settled in Dunquin continued for well over ten years to return to the island two or three times a year to tend and shear their sheep, which they had left there. They used the 'Dáil' (the big house by the 'Yank's Well') as their base. They also used their curraghs, often with mainland-born friends, to ferry the occasional summer visitor or camper across to the island. It was a period of gentle decline, in which rabbits came back to the village and seals appeared on the White Strand in the early autumn.

In 1970 an American visitor, Taylor Collings, inspired by the magnificent scenic backdrop of the island in the film *Ryan's Daughter,* made his way there and immediately became seized with the idea of developing it as his 'Great Blasket Island Ranch'. With great vigour he set about acquiring as many of the island properties as he could, even those that were complete ruins, paying several hundred punts for each one. 'Pennies from heaven!'

Not all the ex-islanders were willing to sell their family inheritance, but within a year Taylor Collings had acquired more than half of all the village holdings. He repaired the two-storey 'government' house at the top of the village and opened it as a guesthouse. He was also able to establish a new water supply from the 'Blind Well' above the village, and built showers and flush toilets alongside his guesthouse.

However, after an active summer season in 1972, Taylor Collings lost interest in the venture. Mr Peter Callery, a member of the firm of Dingle solicitors he had used in buying island properties, now acted as his agent. Year by year enthusiastic 'Blasketophiles' – American, English, French, German and Irish – were engaged to run the guesthouse, and also, eventually, a cafe and youth hostel for the use of visitors. It seemed as if the island was returning to the decay of the previous twenty years, but with the advantage now of basic facilities for visitors, whose numbers steadily increased. The curraghs manned by ex-islanders and their mainland friends, which in the 1960s brought occasional summer visitors (including ourselves) to the island, were replaced by well-equipped, engine-driven ferry boats.

However, the 'free-for-all' that had characterised the use of the island for so many years now had not seemed a satisfactory state of affairs to many of those who had come to know and love the island. This place of outstanding natural beauty and unique historical and literary interest deserved something better. From the early 1970s onwards there were those who urged on successive Irish governments the need to make it a Historic National Park, under a unified, publicly-accountable administration. There are examples worldwide of the practicability and success of such parks. But pleas for action fell on deaf ears until 1985.

In that year came a bombshell. In the name of Taylor Collings the Great Blasket Island was offered for sale in the *Wall Street Journal*, for one million dollars. The possibility, foreseen by some, that the island might become private property, with access denied to the general public, seemed an immediate danger.

This advertisement, and the publicity given to it by the Irish press, quickly led to the setting up of the Blasket Island Foundation and its vigorous campaign, both locally and nationally, for the island to be made an Irish National Park. That campaign received widespread support and led eventually to the passing of the Great Blasket Island National Park Act in 1989, with all-party support in the Dáil.

However, once the Office of Public Works (OPW) tried to implement the Act, by applying its compulsory purchase provisions, the constitutional validity of the Act was challenged in the courts by Mr Peter Callery, to whom, it emerged, Taylor Collings had transferred the titles to his island holdings. After years of expensive litigation, the Act itself was ruled to be unconstitutional, and therefore 'fell'.

In many ways this signalled a return to the Island's post-evacuation pre-1985 situation, except that it had become clear that the Great Blasket island, as an entity, could *not* be bought or sold, as it did not have a single owner (and never had had since 1922).

In the meantime, the opening in 1993 of the Blasket Centre on the mainland just north of Dunquin gave a further impetus to interest in the island and its history. Its excellent display of photographs and other memorabilia of the island, with a varied exhibition of especially commissioned works of art and films, has brought to it over 50,000 visitors a year, many of whom have thereby been encouraged to visit the island itself.

In the year 2000 the legal deadlock with regard to the island was broken by an initiative of the then Minister for Arts, Heritage, Gaeltacht and the Islands, Síle De Valera, when she appointed Martin Nolan, the Manager for Kerry County Council, to chair a Blasket Island Forum, to explore possible ways forward.

Through a series of public meetings and consultations he brought together, and caused to speak to each other, people representing every point of view on the right way forward for the future of the island; in particular, all the owners of private property on the island, and those who had campaigned for it to become a National Park. Nolan carefully analysed and listed the points of general agreement and disagreement, and recommended that a Great Blasket Management Group be set up with the remit of devising a constitution for a public-private executive to manage the island in the future. This recommendation was accepted, and early in

2002 such a group was called into being under the leadership of officers from the OPW and Kerry County Council.

In the submissions made to the forum by people from all over the world, as well as Ireland itself – not least from the families of ex-islanders now living in the USA – it was notable how much support there still was for the view that the island should become a national park, in principle if not in law.

Concurrently, Kerry County Council considered the background conditions appropriate to the island's future, with regard to all the legislation, local, national and European, currently in force, and in 2003 published its own impressive Development Plan for the island, laying down detailed policies to be adopted with regard to the upkeep and restoration of the buildings of the village, its walls and roadways, and policies to be introduced and observed for the protection of wildlife and so on. The thrust of the report was 'Maximum Conservation; Minimum Development'. These policies, if strictly followed, should lead to the Great Blasket Island eventually gaining World Heritage Status.

Late in 2004, after nearly three years' work, the Interim Management Group submitted the final draft of its report, covering the issues raised by Martin Nolan, to the Irish Government. After various further consultations an announcement was made on 8 July 2005, by the Minister for Environment, Heritage and Local Government, Dick Roche, that 'the Government is to proceed with the purchase of An Blascaod Mór.' He looked forward over the next number of years to the implementation of the detailed management plan submitted to him. The Department of Community, Rural and Gaeltacht Affairs was to be responsible for overseeing the work on the improvement of the piers, and the OPW was to have ongoing responsibility for the future promotion, conservation and management of the Island.

This was a truly historic announcement, and, it is to be hoped, marks the key turning point in the island's history in modern times. Indeed, it is the most significant event since the decision to evacuate the island in 1953. It should bring to an end the uneasy 'free-for-all' that characterised the second half of the twentieth century.

It will become, if not in legal title, yet in reality, a 'de facto' national park, which is what lovers of the island have campaigned for for the last twenty years – ever since, in fact, Taylor Collings offered it for sale in the *Wall Street Journal*.

What are the chief challenges that the OPW has to meet as it takes over major responsibility for the future of the island?

The first, I believe, is to restore that sense of warm welcome and friendship and easy co-operation that characterised the island in its Golden Age, and is so clearly celebrated in the writings of the islanders and their visiting scholarly friends. This, in practical terms, means having the minimum of regulations; such 'rules' that have to be made, with regard to litter for example, should be user-friendly. Secondly, it will also mean ensuring a reliable water supply, with drinking, washing and toilet facilities available in the village. There should also continue to be available to visitors simple, reasonably priced refreshments and over-night accommodation, open throughout the summer season without fail. Thirdly, there needs to be a continuation of the safe and reliable ferry service to and from the mainland.

On the island itself, during the summer months, there need to be at hand well-trained rangers, who will offer information and friendly advice to visitors when asked, but will never be officious.

The OPW will have other important responsibilities with regard to the conservation of the village: keeping the use of machinery to an absolute minimum; establishing an effective system of waste disposal, and ensuring the protection of the island's fragile ecological features. All these points are carefully listed in the excellent Development Plan published by the Kerry County Council in 2003.

Finally, the new Management Committee, under the leadership of the OPW, will need to look outwards for comments and suggestions from all the new agencies that have become involved in responsibility for the island's future. The Blasket Centre, Kerry County Council, its Planning Committee, voluntary agencies with a concern for ecological, historical or cultural issues. All have their parts to play. As indeed have the visitors who have discovered this uniquely beautiful and historic island. Your comments and suggestions, dear reader, if passed on to those in authority, can have their part in ensuring the Great Blasket Island has a glorious future, gaining for it eventually the World Heritage Status it so richly deserves.

Notes

CHAPTER 1 – NEXT PARISH AMERICA

1   J. B. Whittow, *Geology and Scenery in Ireland* (Harmondsworth: Penguin Books, 1974), p.207.

CHAPTER 2 – ORIGINS OF THE ISLAND COMMUNITY

2   Peter Harbison, *Guide to the National Monuments of Ireland* (Dublin: Gill and MacMillan, 1970).
3. Tomás Ó Criomhthain, *Dinnsheanchas na mBlascaodaí* (Dublin, 1935), p.21.
4   W. Spotswood Green, "Armada Ships on the Kerry Coast", *Proceedings of the Royal Irish Academy* 27 (1901). The letter from James Trent to Sir Edward Denny is contained in the *Calendar of State Papers relating to the defeat of the Spanish Armada, 1588,* ed. Sir John Laughton (London, 1894).
5   Colin Martin, *Full Fathom Five* (London: Chatto and Windus, 1975), p.54.
6   "The Knight of Glin, Lord Orrery's Travels in Kerry", *Journal of the Kerry Archaeological and Historical Society* 5 (1972).
7   Charles Smith, *The Ancient and Present State of the County of Kerry* (1756).
8   Ibid.

CHAPTER 3 – THE ISLAND FAMILIES

9   Maurice O'Sullivan, *Twenty Years A-Growing* (London, 1933).
10 John Millington Synge, *In Wicklow and West Kerry* (Dublin: Maunsel and Co., 1912).
11 Two boys, probably twins, were baptised in 1868. The mother's name is given as Ellen Landers. This may represent a clerical error, however, since another entry a few lines above lists Ellen Landers as the wife of Michael Kane.
12 John Millington Synge, *In Wicklow and West Kerry* (Dublin: Maunsel and Co., 1912), p.94.

CHAPTER 4 – THE BLASKETS DURING THE FAMINE

13 Bernard H. Becker, *Disturbed Ireland* (1880), p.233.
14 *Annual Report of the Dingle and Ventry Mission Association for the year ending December 1847* (Dublin, 1848), Royal Irish Academy, Halliday pamphlets, p.11.
15 Ibid.
16 Ibid.
17 *Annual Report of the Dingle and Ventry Mission Association for the year ending December 1850* (Dublin, 1851), Royal Irish Academy, Halliday pamphlets, p.15.
18 *Annual Report of the Irish Society of London for the year ending December 1851* (London, 1852).
19 Tomás Ó Criomhthain, *An tOileánach* (Dublin, 1929), p.12. The English version is found in *The Islandman* (Dublin: Talbot Press, 1937), p.10.

20 *Tralee Chronicle* 21 December 1850.
21 *Annual Report of the Dingle and Ventry Mission Association for the year ending December 1850* (Dublin, 1851), Royal Irish Academy, Halliday pamphlets, p.16.
22 *Tralee Chronicle* 13 January 1854.

CHAPTER 5 — THE HARBOUR

23 *Annual Report of the Congested Districts Board, Ireland* (London, 1893).
24 Mrs. A. M. Thompson, *A Brief Account in the Change in Religious Opinion . . . in Dingle and the West of Kerry* (London, 1846), pp. 95, 97, 104 ff.
25 T. F. O'Sullivan, *Romantic Hidden Kerry* (Tralee, 1931), p.578.
26 *Tralee Chronicle* 11 and 18 September 1847.
27 *Tralee Chronicle* 13 January 1854.
28 Sam Hussey, *Reminiscences of an Irish Land Agent* (London, 1904).
29 John Millington Synge, *In Wicklow and West Kerry* (Dublin: Maunsel and Co., 1912).
30 Tomás Ó Criomhthain, *Dinnsheanchas na mBlascaodaí* (Dublin, 1935).

CHAPTER 6 — THE ISLAND VILLAGE AND ITS HOUSES

31 See, for example, John Windele's description of the clochán on Inis Tuaisceart in which a family was living in 1838. Padraig de Brun, "John Windele and Father Casey", *Journal of the Kerry Archaeological and Historical Society* 7 (1974): 96-97, 101.
32 This population figure is found in a letter from Tomás Ó Criomhthain to Robin Flower dated 16 October 1916 which is quoted in *Seanchas ón Oileán Tiar*, ed. Seamus Ó Duilearga (Dublin, 1956), p.262.
33 Maurice Ó Sullivan, *Twenty Years A-Growing* (London, 1933), p.109.
34 Tomás Ó Criomhthain, *The Islandman* (Dublin: Talbot Press, 1937), p.2.
35 See J. M. Synge's account of the King's Kitchen in 1905 contained in *In Wicklow and West Kerry* (Dublin: Maunsel and Co., 1912), pp.90-91.
36 Tomás Ó Criomhthain, *The Islandman* (Dublin: Talbot Press, 1937), p.195. A photograph of a thatched Blasket house appears in Harrison H. Walker, "Old Ireland, Mother of New Eire", *National Geographic Magazine* 77 (1940): 683.
37 Iorweth C. Peake, *The Welsh House* (Liverpool: Brython Press, 1946), pp.174-75 and plates 77, 78.
38 T. F. O'Sullivan, *Romantic Hidden Kerry* (Tralee, 1931), p.307.
39 Tomás Ó Criomhthain, *The Islandman* (Dublin: Talbot Press, 1937), pp.29, 234. Tomás Ó Criomhthain states in one place that the Board built six houses but, elsewhere, that they built five.
40 Arthur Young, *A Tour in Ireland . . . in the years 1776, 1777 and 1778,* ed. C. Maxwell (Cambridge, 1925), p.187.
41 House books of the Griffith Valuation (Parish of Dunquin) are contained in the Public Record Office, Dublin.
42 Congested Districts Board (Estates Department), *Four-Roomed Dwelling Houses* (Dublin: HMSO, 1914).
43 Tomás Ó Criomhthain records that he was paid 2/- per day. Accounts of the building work can be found in *The Islandman* (Dublin: Talbot Press, 1937), pp.233-35; Mícheál Ó Gaoithín, *Is Truaghná Fanaun an Óige* (Dublin, 1953), pp. 4-7; Robin Flower, *The Western Island* (Oxford, 1944), pp. 37-38, 44-46.
44 *Appendix to the Minutes of Evidence . . . to the Devon Commission* (London: HMSO, 1845), part 4, p.56.
45 John Millington Synge, Synge Collection, Trinity College, Dublin, notebook No. 4403.
46 Charles Gayer, *The Persecution of Protestants* (London, 1845). The drawing is also reproduced in *Céad Bháin,* ed. Micheál Ó Ciosáin (Ballyferriter, 1973), p.45.

CHAPTER 8 – THE WILD WEST

47   *Tralee Chronicle* 21 December 1850.
48   *Annual Report of the Dingle and Ventry Mission Association for the year ending December 1850* (Dublin, 1851), Royal Irish Academy, Halliday pamphlets, pp.15-17.
49   *Tralee Chronicle* 13 January 1954.
50   Lydia Jane Fisher, *Letters from the Kingdom of Kerry in 1845* (London, 1846).
51   Ibid., p.78.
52   Lady Henrietta Chatterton, *Rambles in the South of Ireland during 1838,* 2nd ed., (London, 1839), vol. 1, p.183.
53   Joseph Wilson, *Innisfail or the Irish Scripture Reader* (1841), pp.104-05. See also Mrs A. M. Thompson, *A Brief Account in the Change in Religious Opinion . . . in Dingle and the West of Kerry* (London, 1846), pp.104-05.
54   *Annual Report of the Irish Society of London for the year ending December 1843* (London, 1844).
55   John Windele, *Travels in Kerry,* Royal Irish Academy, Dublin, ms. 12, c.11, pp. 132-43. See also Padraig de Brun, "John Windele and Father Casey", *Journal of the Kerry Archaeological and Historical Society* 7 (1974): 101-03.
56   T. F. O'Sullivan, *Romantic Hidden Kerry* (Tralee, 1931), pp.245, 576.
57   Bernard H. Becker, *Disturbed Ireland* (1880), p.232.
58   Sam Hussey, *Reminiscences of an Irish Land Agent* (London, 1904), p.200.
59   John Millington Synge, *In Wicklow and West Kerry* (Dublin: Maunsel, 1912).
60   Peig Sayers, *An Old Woman's Reflections* (London, 1962).
61   *Kerry Evening Post* 13 December 1848.

CHAPTER 9 – THE FLOWERING OF LITERARY TALENT

62   For details see Peig Sayers, *An Old Woman's Reflections* (London, 1962), chapter 17.

CHAPTER 10 – THE OUTER ISLANDS

63   Charles Smith, *The Ancient and Present State of the County of Kerry* (1756).
64   Ibid.
65   John Windele, *Travels in Kerry,* Royal Irish Academy, Dublin, ms. 12, c.11, pp.132-43.
66   George du Noyer, *Proceedings of the Royal Irish Academy* Vol. 8 (1861-64), pp.429ff.
67   Tomás Ó Criomhthain, *The Islandman* (Dublin: Talbot Press, 1937).
68   Robin Flower, *The Western Island* (Oxford, 1944).
69   Ibid.
70   John Millington Synge, *In Wicklow and West Kerry* (Dublin: Maunsel and Co., 1912).
71   We are indebted to Sean and Mauris Guiheen, ex-islanders now living in Dunquin, for the details of this event.
72   Seamus Ó Duilearga (ed.), *Seanchas ón Oileán Tiar* (Dublin, 1956).
73   Padraig de Brun, "John Windele and Father Casey", *Journal of the Kerry Archaeological and Historical Society* 7 (1974).
74   George de Noyer, *Proceedings of the Royal Irish Academy* Vol. 8 (1861-64), pp.429ff.
75   Father Casey's letter is found in the Royal Irish Academy, Dublin, ms. 12, L.5, item 174.
76   Charles Smith, *The Ancient and Present State of the County of Kerry* (1756).

Index